Quick & Easy
Way To Learn German

ARATI NILEN

QUALIS BOOKS

G T BOOK
AGENCY

ISBN: 81-87838-03-5

1st Published in Qualis Books, 2005
Quick & Easy Way to Learn German

Reprinted 2026

Cover design by: The Exact Page

Published by
Qualis Books
140, Medha Apartment
Mayur Vihar, Ext. Phase 1,
New Delhi - 110091
E-mail : qualisbooks@yahoo.co.in

Printed in India at
D.K. Fine Art Press (P) Ltd.
Delhi- 110052

Quick & Easy Way to Learn German

German language is close to English language in its grammatical structure and vocabulary. This book teaches you German, by using English language as a tool, following the easiest and most comprehensive methodology. Broadly this book is divided into three categories: vocabulary, grammar and dialogues. A language is constituted primarily of these three components.

Through this book, you can learn German language with a German taste, as while teaching you German, it provides you a glimpse of the culture of German speaking countries too.

I hope this book will prove helpful to all those who wish to learn German through English.

CONTENTS

Part-I
Chapter 1

German Alphabets

German		Pronunciation
A	[a]	aa
B	[b]	bay
C	[c]	se
D	[d]	de
E	[e]	ay
F	[f]	ef
G	[g]	gay
H	[h]	haa
I	[i]	i
J	[j]	yot
K	[k]	kaa
L	[l]	el
M	[m]	em
N	[n]	en
O	[o]	o
P	[p]	pe
Q	[q]	ku
R	[r]	er
S	[s]	es
T	[t]	tay
U	[u]	u
V	[v]	fau

W	[w]	vay
X	[x]	iks
Y	[y]	ipsilon
Z	[z]	tse
Ä	[ä] (a-Umlaut)	ae
Ö	[ö] (o- Umlaut)	oe
Ü	[ü] (u-Umlaut)	ue
ß	[ss]	s s

Chapter 2

Letters and Sounds

The Sounds of German. The good news about German pronunciation is that there are clear rules about how you pronounce each letter. However, the same as with English, people speak with different accents, depending on their region and background.

Most sounds are recognisable to the English ear, though there are some differences one needs to be aware of.

Vowels

a, e, i, o, u

They can be short or long, depending on where they appear in a word.

Tegel

1. The first **e** is long and similar to the sound in Scottish **gate**.
2. The second **e** is short and similar to the sound in English **Ben**.

Flughafen

1. The **u** is short, similar to the sound in English **put**.
2. The **a** is long, similar to the sound in English **half**.
3. The **e** is short, similar to the sound in English **Ben**.

Hoffmann

1. The **o** is short, similar to the sound in English **shop**.
2. The **a** is short, similar to the sound in Northern English **man**.

Sind, bin

1. The **i** is short, similar to the sound in English **bin**.

Vowel Combinations

Sie

The **ie** is pronounced like 'ee' as in English **see**.

Claus

The **au** always sounds like 'ow' as in English **how**.

Freut mich

The **eu** always sounds like 'oy' as in English **boy**.

Neddermeyer

The **ey** / **ei** / **ay** / **ai** combinations are always pronounced like eye in English.

Consonants

Ich auch

1. The **ch** sounds a bit like the 'h' in English huge after i.
2. But ch is harder after au - more like the 'ch' in Scottish loch.

Sind Sie Claus?

1. The **s** always sounds like an English 'z' at the beginning of a word.
2. But at the end of a word it always sounds like an English s.

Willkommen

1. The **w** always sounds like the English letter 'v'.
2. In contrast, **v** is normally pronounced like the English letter 'f'.

Tegel, Guten Tag

1. The **g** is always hard like the English **guest**.

Freut mich

The **r** is pronounced quite differently from the standard English 'r'. It's a more guttural sound, pronounced at the back of the throat in standard German, but it tends to be silent at the end of words. In Southern Germany you may hear it pronounced as a trill.

Ja

1. The **j** is always pronounced like the English 'y'.
2. Vowel: a, e, i, o, u

Long Vowel Sounds

		German	Pronunciation	English
a	—	Vater	faatar	father
e	—	zehn	tsayn	ten
i	—	wir	vear	we
ie		die	dee	the
c	—	Brot	brot	bread
u	—	Schule	shoolay	School
ä	—	zählen	tsaelayn	to count
ö	—	hören	hoerayn	to hear
ü	—	fühlen	fuehlen	to feel

Short Vowel Sounds

		German	Pronunciation	English
a	—	Mann	maan	man
e	—	Wetter	vetayr	weather
i	—	Winter	vinter	winter
o	—	Onkel	onkel	uncle
u	—	Butter	bootar	butter
ä	—	März	maerts	March
ö	—	zwölf	tswoelf	twelve
ü	—	füllen	fuelen	to fill

Consonant Sounds Needing Special Attention

v	—	f voll (fol)
j	—	(like y in young) jung
s	—	Glas (glaas)
s s	—	Wasser
ß	—	Fuß
Sch	—	Schuh
sp (initial)	—	spielen
st (initial)	—	stehen
ch (front)	—	ich, nicht (ix, nixt)
ch (back)	—	acht, Buch (akht, bukh)

b, d, g at the end of a word:

d > t Kind (kint) child

b > p Jakob (Ja-kop)

g > k except after **i**, where **g** becomes front **ch**

ig > ich fertig (fer-tix) finished

ag > ak Tag (Taak) day

eg > ek Weg (weeg) way

Chapter 3

Basic Expressions

English	German	Pronunciation
Good Morning	Guten Morgen	gutayn morgayn
Good Afternoon	Guten Mittag	gutayn mitaak
Good Evening	Guten Abend	gutayn aabent
Good Night	Gute Nacht	gute naakht
Hello/Good Day	Guten Tag	guten taak
Thank you	Danke	Daankay
Excuse me	Entschuldigen Sie	entschooldigen zee
I am sorry	Tut mir leid	toot mear laait
Please	Bitte	beetay
How are you?	Wie geht es?	vee gayht es?
Fine, Thank you	Gut, Danke	gut, dankay
And you?	Und Sie?	unt zee?
Cheers!	Prost!	prost!
See you	Aufwiedersehen	aufviderzehen
Yes	Ja	yaa
No	Nein	nine

Part-II
Chapter 1

Parts of Human Body

Der menschliche Körperteil:-
dayr menshlishe koerpertaail

English	German	Pronunciation
Ankle	(der) Knöchel	knoekhayl
Arm	(der) Arm	arm
Back	(der) Rücken	ryookayn
Beard	(der) Bart	baart
Blood	(das) Blut	bloot
Body	(der) Körper	koerpayr
Chest/breast	(die) Brust	broost
Cheek	(die) Wange	vangay
Chin	(das) Kinn	kinn
Ear	(das) Ohr	ohr
Elbow	(der) Ellenbogen	aylenbogayn
Eye	(das) Auge	aaoogay
Eyeball	(der) Augenapfel	aaoogaynapfel
Eyebrow	(die) Augenbraue	aaoogaynbraau
Eyelash	(die) Augenwimper	aaoogaynwimper

Eyelid	(das) Augenlid	aaoogaynlid
Eyesight	(das) Augenlicht	aaoogaynlisht
Face	(das) Gesicht	gayzisht
Finger	(der) Finger	feengayr
Fist	(die) Faust	faaost
Flesh	(das) Fleisch	flaaish
Forhead	(die) Stirne	estirnay
Hair	(das) Haar	haar
Hand	(die) Hand	haant
Head	(der) Kopf	kopf
Heart	(das) Herz	herts
Hip	(die) Hüfte	hueftay
Knee	(das) Knie	knee (k is pronounced)
Leg	(das) Bein	baain
Lips	(die) Lippe	lipay
Moustache	(der) Schnurrbart	shnoorbaart
Mouth	(der) Mund	moont
Nail	(der) Nagel	naagayl
Neck	(der) Hals	haals
Nose	(die) Nase	naazay
Palm	(die) Handfläche	haandflaekhay
Shoulder	(die) Schulter	shooltayr
Skin	(die) Haut	haaut

Skull	(der) Schädel	shaedayl
Sole	(die) Sohle	zolay
Spine	(die) Wirbelsäule	virbaylzaeulay
Stomach	(der) Magen	maagayn
Thigh	(der) Oberschenkel	obayrshenkel
Throat	(die) Kehle	kayhlay
Thumb	(der) Daumen	doumayn
Tongue	(die) Zunge	tsoongay
Tooth	(der) Zahn	tsaan
Vein	(die) Ader	aadayr
Waist	(die) Taille	taailay
Wrist	(das) Handgelenk	haantgaylaynk

Chapter 2

Animals, Birds, Insects

Tiere, Vögel, Insekten (teeferay, foegel, inzektayn)

TIERE

English	German	Pronunciation
Animal	(das) Tier	tear
Bull	(die) Bulle	bulay
Bitch	(die) Hündin	huendin
Camel	(das) Kamel	kaamel
Calf	(das) Kalb	kaalb
Cat	(die) Katze	kaatsay
Chameleon	(das) Chamäleon	shamaeleon
Cow	(die) Kuh	ku
Crab	(die) Krabbe	kraabay
Crocodile	(das) Krokodil	krokodeel
Deer	(der) Hirsch	hirsh
Dog	(der) Hund	hoont
Donkey	(der) Esel	ezel
Elephant	(der) Elefant	Elefaant
Fish	(der) Fisch	fish
Fox	(der) Fuchs	fookhs

Goat	(die) Ziege	tseegay
Hare	(der) Hase	haazay
Horse	(das) Pferd	ferd
Jackal	(der) Schakal	shakaal
Lamb	(das) Laam	laam
Leech	(der) Blutegel	blootegel
Lion	(der) Löwe	loevay
Lioness	(die) Löwin	loevin
Mare	(die) Stüte	stuetay
Monkey	(der) Affe	aafe
Mouse	(die) Mous	mouse
Pig	(das) Schwein	shvaain
Pup	(der) junge Hund	yungay hoont
Sheep	(das) Schaf	shaaf
Snake	(die) Schlange	shlaangay
Squirrel	(das) Eichhörnchen	aayishhoernshen
Tiger	(der) Tiger	teegar
Tortoise	(die) Schildkröte	shiltkroetay
Wolf	(der) Wolf	volf

VÖGEL

English	German	Pronunciation
Bird	(der) Vogel	fogel
Cock	(der) Hahn	haan
Crow	(die) Krähe	kraehay
Cuckoo	(der) Kuckuck	kukuk
Dove	(die) Taube	taaubay
Hen	(die) Henne	haynay
Nightingale	(die) Nachtigall	naakhtigal
Parrot	(der) Papagei	paapaagayee
Peacock	(der) Pfau	pfaao
Pigeon	(die) Taube	taaubay
Sparrow	(der) Sperling	spayrling
Swan	(der) Schwan	shvaan
Vulture	(der) Geier	gayer
Owl	(die) Eule	aulay

INSEKTEN

English	German	Pronunciation
Ant	(die) Ameise	amaayezay
Bee	(die) Biene	beenay
Bug	(die) Wanze	vantsay
Butterfly	(der) Schmetterling	shmeterling
Fly	(die) Fliege	fleegay
Frog	(der) Frosch	frosh
Insect	(das) Insekt	inzekt
Lizard	(die) Eidechse	aaidekhsay
Mosquito	(der) Moskito	moskito
Spider	(die) Spinne	shpinay
Snail	(die) Schneke	shnekay
Wasp	(die) Wespe	vespay

Chapter 3

Food

Essen:-
esayn

English	German	Pronunciation
Apple	(der) Apfel	aapfel
Apricot	(die) Aprikose	aaprikoze
Aubergine	(die) Aubergine	aubayrginay
Banana	(die) Banane	banaana
Bean	(die) Bohne	bohnay
Beef	(das) Rindfleisch	rindflaaish
Beer	(das) Bier	beear
Bill (in restaurant)	(die) Rechnung	raykhnung
Biscuit	(der) Keks	kayks
Beverage	(das) Getränk	getraenk
Blackberry	(die) Brombeere	brombaray
Bread	(das) Brot	brot
Breakfast	(das) Frühstück	frueshtuek
Butter	(die) Butter	butar
Cabbage	(der) Kohl	kol
Cake	(der) Kuchen	kukhayn
Can	(die) Dose	dozay

Cauliflower	(der) Blumenkohl	bloomenkol
Cheese	(der) Käse	kaeze
Cherry	(die) Kirsche	kirshay
Chicken	(das) Hähnchen	haenshayn
Chocolate	(die) Schokolade	shokolaade
Cider	(der) Apfelwein	aapfaylwein
Coffee	(der) Kaffee	kaafay
Cream	(die) Sahne	zaanay
Cup	(die) Tasse	taasay
Dessert	(die) Nachspeise	naakhshpeizay
Dinner/supper	(das) Abendessen	aabentesen
Egg	(das) Ei	aaee
Flour	(das) Mehl	mayl
Fork	(die) Gabel	gaabayl
Fresh	Frisch *(adj.)*	frish
Fruit	(die) Frucht	frukht
Frying pan	(die) Pfanne	pfaanay (p will be pronounced)
Garlic	(der) Knoblauch	knoblaaukh (both k will be pronounced)
Glass	(das) Glas	glaas
Grape	(die) Traube	traaubay
Ham	(der) Schinken	shinken

Honey	(der) Honig	honig
Hot drink	(das) Heißgetränk	haais gaytraenk
Jug/Mug	(der) Krug	krug
Juice	(der) Saft	zaaft
Knife	(das) Messer	maysar
Lamb	(das) Lammfleisch	laamflaaish
Lemonade	(die) Limonade	limonaaday
Lemon	(die) Zitrone	tsitronay
Lunch	(das) Mittagessen	mitaakesen
Main course	(das) Hauptgericht	hauptgerikht
Meat	(das) Fleisch	flaaish
Melon	(die) Melone	maylone
Menu	(die) Speisekarte	shpaizakarte
Milk	(die) Milch	milsh
Mustard	(der) Senf	zenf
Nut	(die) Nuss	noos
Oil	(das) Öl	oel
Onion	(die) Zwiebel	tsveebayl
Pan	(der) Topf	topf (p will be pronounced)
Pea	(die) Erbse	erbsay
Pear	(die) Birne	birnay
Peach	(der) Pfirsich	pfirzish (p will be pronounced)

Pepper	der Pfeffer	pfayfar (p will be pronounced)
Pineapple	(die) Ananas	anaanas
Plate	(der) Teller	telar
Plum	(die) Pflaume	pflaaumay (p will be pronounced)
Pork	(das) Schweinefleisch	shvaainflaaish
Potato	(die) Kartoffel	kaartofal
Raisin	(die) Rosine	rozinay
Raspberry	(die) Himbeere	himbeeray
Raw	roh *(adj.)*	roh
Rice	(der) Reis	raais (pronounced as in English)
Salad	(der) Salat	zalaat
Salt	(das) Salz	zaalts (t will be pronounced)
Sauce/dressing	(die) Soße	zosay
Saucer	(die) Untertasse	untartaasay
Sausage	(die) Wurst	woorst
Soft/tender	zart (*adj.*)	tsaart
Soup	(die) Suppe	zoopay
Sour/sharp	sauer (adj.)	zaauar
Spice	(das) Gewürz	gaywuerts
Spicy/sharp	scharf (*adj.*)	shaarf

Spinach	(der) Spinat	shpinaat
Spoon	(der) Löffel	loefal
Starter	(die) Vorspeise	forspaaizay
Steak	(das) Steak	steek
Strawberry	(die) Erdbeere	erdbeeray
Sugar	(der) Zucker	tsukar
Sweet	süß (*adj*)	zues
Tea	(der) Tee	tay
Tomato	(die) Tomate	tomaatay
Vegetables	(das) Gemüse	gaymuezay
Vinegar	(der) Essig	essig
Wheat	(der) Weizen	vaaitsayn
Wine	(der) Wein	wine (as in English)

Chapter 4

Home

Wohnung:-
vohnung

English	German	Pronunciation
Above	oben	obayn
Alarm clock	(der) Wecker	veker
Apartment	(die) Wohnung	vohnung
Armchair	(der) Sessel	zesayl
Attic	(der) Dachboden	daakhbodayn
Balcony	(der) Balkon	baalkon
Bathroom	(das) Badezimmer	baadaytsimar
Bed	(das) Bett	bet
Bedroom	(das) Schlafzimmer	shlaaftsimar
Bedsheet	(das) Laken	laakayn
Below	unten	oonten
Blanket/Quilt	(die) Bettdecke	betdayke
Broom/Brush	(der) Besen	bayzayn
Bucket	(der) Eimer	aaimayr
Bungalow	(der) Bungalow	bungalow (as in English

Carpet	(der) Teppich	taypish
Ceiling	(die) Decke	dayke
Centralheating	(die) Zentralheizung	tsentraalhaaitsung (t will be pronounced)
Chair	(der) Stuhl	stul
Chest of drawers	(die) Kommode	komode
Chimney	(der) Kamin	kaamin
Clean	sauber *(adj.)*	zaaubayr
Cloth/rag	(der) Lappen	laapayn
Cold	kalt *(adj.)*	kaalt
Cooker	(der) Herd	hayrt
Cosy	gemütlich (adj.)	gemuetlish
Cupboard	(der) Schrank	shraank
Curtain	(der)Vorhang	forhaang
Cushion	(das) Kissen	kisayn
Damp	feucht *(adj.)*	feukt
Dark	dunkel *(adj.)*	dunkayl
Desk	(der) Schreibtisch	shraaibtish
Diningroom	(das) Esszimmer	estsimar
Dirt/filth	(der) Schmutz	shmoots
Dishwasher	(die)Spülmaschine	shpuelmaashinay
Door	(die) Tür	tuer
Doormat	(die) Fußmatte	foosmaatay

Draughty	zugig *(adj.)*	tsugig (t will be pronounced)
Drawer	(die) Schublade	shuhblaade
Dressingtable	(die) Frisierkommode	frizierkomode
Dry	trocken (adj.)	troken
Dust	(der) Staub	shtaaub
Dustbin	(der) Mülleimer	muelaaimayr
Fence	(der) Zaun	tsaaun (t will be pronounced)
Floor/ground	(der) Boden	bodayn
Furniture	(die) Möbel	moebayl
Garage	(die) Garage	garaajay
Garden	(der) Garten	gaartan
Grand	großartig *(adj.)*	grosaartik
Heater	(der) Heizkörper	haaitskoerpayr
House	(das) Haus	house
Iron	(das) Bügeleisen	buegaylaaizayn
Kettle	(der) Kessel	kaysayl
Key	(der) Schlüssel	shluesayl
Kitchen	(die) Küche	kueshe
Kitchen sink	(die) Spüle	shpuelay
Lawn	(der) Rasen	raazayn
Light/bright/clear	hell *(adj.)*	hel
Livingroom	(das) Wohnzimmer	vohntsimar

Lock	(das) Schloss	shlos
Microwave	(die) Mikrowelle	mikrovaylay
Mirror	(der) Spiegel	speegayl
Mop	(der) Mopp	mop
Neighbour (male)	(der)Nachbar	naakhbaar
Old-fashioned	altmodisch (*adj.)*	aaltmodish
Picture	(das) Bild	bilt
Pillow	(das) Kopfkissen	kopfkisayn
Radio	(das) Radio	raadio
Refrigrator	(der) Kühlschrank	kuelshraank
Roof	(das) Dach	daakh
Shampoo	(das) Shampoo	shampoo
Shed	(der) Schuppen	shupayn
Shelf	(das) Regal	regaal
Shower	(die) Dusche	dushay
Shutter	(der) Fensterladen	fenstarlaadayn
Soap	(die) Seife	zaaifay
Sofa	(das) Sofa	sofa (as in English)
Spacious	geräumig (adj.)	geraeumik
Stool	(der) Hocker	hokayr
Staircase	(die) Treppe	traypay
Study	(das) Arbeitszimmer	aarbaaitstsimar
Switch	(der)Lichtschalter	lishtshaaltayr
Table	(der) Tisch	tish

Telephone	(das) Telefon	telephone (as in English)
Television	(der) Fernseher	fernzayar
Tidy/neat	ordentlich *(adj.)*	ordayntlish
Toilet	(die) Toilette	toilaytay
To renovate	renovieren *v.*	renovieren
To repair	reparieren *v.*	raypaarierayn
Toothpaste	(die) Zahnpasta	tsaanpaasta (t will be pronounced)
Towel	(das) Handtuch	haandtukh
Untidy	unordentlich *(adj.)*	oonordayntish
Vacuumcleaner	(der)Staubsauger	shtaaubsaugayr
Vase	(die) Vase	vaas
Videorecorder	(der)Videorekorder	videorecorder (as in English)
Wall	(die) Wand	vaant
Wall (eterior)	(die) Mauer	maauayr
Wallpaper	(die) Tapete	taapaytay
Wardrobe	(der) Kleiderschrank	klaaidayrshraank
Warm	warm (adj.)	vaarm
Washbasin	(das) Waschbecken	waashbaykayn
Washingmachine	(die) Waschmaschine	vaashmaashinay
Wet	nass *(adj.)*	naas
Window	(das) Fenster	fenstar
Window sill	(die) Fensterbank	fenstarbaank

Chapter 5

Clothing

Kleidung:-
klaaidung

English	German	Pronunciation
Belt	(der) Gürtel	guertayl
Black	schwarz *(adj)*	shwaarts
Blouse	(die) Bluse	bloozay
Blue	blau *(adj.)*	blaau
Boot	(der) Stiefel	shtifayl
Bracelet	(das) Armband	aarmbaant
Brown	braun *(adj.)*	braaun
Button	(der) Knopf	knopf (k, p will be pronounced)
Cap	(die) Mütze	muetsay
Chain	(die) Kette	kete
Coat	(der) Mantel	maantayl
Collar	(der) Kragen	kraagayn
Colour	(die) Farbe	faarbay
Comfortable	bequem *(adj.)*	baykvaym
Costume	(das) Kostüm	kostuem
Cotton	(die) Baumwolle	baaumvolay

Dye	(der) Farbstoff	faarbstof
Earring	(der) Ohrring	orring
Fashion	(die) Mode	moday
Fur	(der) Pelz	paylts
Garment	(das)Kleid	klaaid
Glove	(der) Handschuh	haantshuh
Green	grün *(adj.)*	gruen
Grey	grau *(adj.)*	graau
Handbag	(die) Handtasche	haanttaashay
Handkerchief	(das) Taschentuch	tashayntukh
Hat	(der) Hut	hoot
Jacket	(die) Jacke	yaakay
Jeans	(die) Jeans	Jeans (as in English)
Jewellery	(der) Schmuck	shmuk
Knickers	(der) Schlüpfer	shluepfayr
Leather	(das) Leder	laydayr
Linen	(das) Leinen	laainayn
Lingerie	(die)Unterwäsche	untayrvayshay
Lipstick	(der) Lippenstift	lipaynshtift
Long	lang *(adj.)*	laang
Make-up	(das) Make-up	make-up (as in English)
Needle	(die) Nadel	naadayl

Nightdress	(das) Nachthemd	naakhthemt
Nude	nackt	naakt
Nylon	(das) Nylon	nylon (as in English)
Orange	orange	oraanzay
Pair	(das) Paar	paar
Perfume	(das) Parfüm	paarfuem
Pocket	(die) Tasche	taashay
Pullover	(der) Pullover	pulover
Purse	(der) Geldbeutel	geltbeutayl
Pyjamas	(der) Schlafanzug	shlaafantsug
Raincoat	(der)Regenmantel	regenmaantayl
Red	rot (*adj.)*	rot
Ring	(der) Ring	ring
Sandal	(die) Sandale	zaandaalay
Satin	(der) Satin	zaatin
Scarf	(der) Schal	shaal
Sewingmachine	(die) Nähmaschine	naehmaashinay
Shirt	(das) Hemd	hemt
Shoe	(der) Schuh	shuh
Short	kurz (*adj.*)	kurts
Shorts	(die) Shorts	shorts (as in English)
Silk	(die) Seide	zaaiday
Size	(die) Größe	groesay

Skirt	(der) Rock	rock
Sleeve	(der) Ärmel	aermayl
Slipper	(der) Hausschuh	houseshuh
Sock	(die) Socke	zokay
Spectacles	(die) Brille	brilay
Stocking	(der) Strumpf	strumpf
Suit	(der) Anzug	aantsug
Sunglasses	(die) Sonnenbrille	zonaynbrilay
Swimsuit	(der) Badeanzug	baadaynantsug
Tie	(die) Krawatte	kravaatay
Tracksuit	(der) Jogginganzug	Joggingantsug
Trousers	(die) Hose	hozay
Umbrella	(der) Schirm	shirm
Underpants	(die) Unterhose	untayrhozay
Uniform	(die) Uniform	ooniform
Velvet	(der) Samt	zaamt
Vest	(das) Unterhemd	untayrhemt
Waistcoat	(die) Weste	vaystay
Wallet	(die) Brieftasche	breeftaashay
White	weiß *(adj.)*	vaais
Wool	(die) Wolle	volay
Yellow	gelb *(adj.)*	gelb

Chapter 6

Health

Gesundheit:-
gezunthaait

English	German	Pronunciation
Accident	(der) Unfall	oonfaal
Allergy	(die) Allergie	alergee
Ambulance	(der) Krankenwagen	kraankaynvaagayn
Appointment	(der) Termin	termin
Asthma	(das) Asthma	asthma (as in English)
Bandage	(der) Verband	ferbaant
Blister	(die) Blase	blaazay
Blood	(das) Blut	bloot
Blood pressure	(der) Blutdruck	blootdruk
Boil	(der/das) Furunkel	fooroonkayl
Cold	(die) Erkältung	erkaeltung
Condom	(der/das) Kondom	condom (as in English)
Constipation	(die) Verstopfung	fershtopfung
Contraceptive	(das) Verhütungsmittel	erhuetungsmitayl
Crutch	(die) Krücke	Kruekay

Cure	(das) Heilmittel	haailmitayl
Cut	(der) Schnitt	shnit
Diabetes	(die) Zuckerkrankheit	tsukarkraankhaait
Diagnosis	(die) Diagnose	diyaagnozay
Dose	(die) Dosis	dosis
Drug	(die) Droge	drogay
Epidemic	(die) Epidemie	epidaymee
Health	(die) Gesundheit	gezunthaait
Healthy	gesund *(adj.)*	gezunt
Heartbeat	(der)Herzschlag	hertsshlaag
Illness	(die) Krankheit	kraankenhaait
Influenza	(die) Grippe	gripay
Injection	(die) Spritze	shpritsay
Injury	(die) Verletzung	ferletsung (t will be pronounced)
Kidney	(die) Niere	neeray
Liver	(die) Leber	laybayr
Medicine	(die) Medizin	meditsin
Nutrition	(die) Ernährung	ernaehrung
Operation	(die) Operation	operatsion
Pain	(der) Schmerz	shmayrts (t *will* be pronounced)
Painkiller	(das) Schmerzmittel	shmayrtsmitel
Patient	(der) Patient	paatseeaynt
Pimple	(der) Pickel	pikayl

Poison	(das) Gift	gift (as in English)
Prescription	(das) Rezept	retsept (t will be pronounced)
Pulse	(der) Puls	pools
Scar	(die)Narbe	naarbe
Sexual organ	(das) Geschlechtsorgan	gayshlaysht-sorgaan
Sick	krank *(adj.)*	kraank
Side effect	(die) Nebenwirkung	naybaynvirkung
Skeleton	(das) Skelett	skaylayt
Surgery	(die) Chirurgie	shirurgee
Sweat	(der) Schweiß	shvaais
Tablet	(die) Tablette	taablaytay
Temple	(die) Schläfe	shlaefay
Thermometer	(das) Thermometer	thermometer
Treatment	(die) Behandlung	bayhaandlung
Vaccination	(die) Impfung	impfung (p will be pronounced)
Weak	schwach *(adj.)*	shwaakh
Wheelchair	(der) Rollstuhl	rolstul

Chapter 7

Nature

Natur:-
naatuar (t will be pronunced)

English	German	Pronunciation
Air	(die) Luft	luft
Atmosphere	(die) Atmosphäre	atmosfaeray
Avalanche	(die) Lawine	laavinay
Bay	(die) Bucht	bukht
Branch	(der) Ast	aast
Breeze	(die) Brise	brizay
Climate	(das) Klima	klimaa
Cloud	(die)Wolke	volkay
Coast, shore	(die) Küste	kuestay
Constellation	(das) Sternbild	shternbilt
Continent	(der) Kontinent	continent (as in English)
Desert	(die) Wüste	vuestay
Drizzle	(der) Nieselregen	neezaylraygayn
Earth	(die) Erde	erday
Earthquake	(das) Erdbeben	erdlaybayn
Fire	(das) Feuer	foyar

Flood	(die) Überschwemmung	uebayrshwaymung
Flower	(die) Blume	bloomay
Forest	(der) Wald	waalt
Frost	(der) Frost	frost
Grass	(das) Gras	graas
Hail	(der) Hagel	haagayl
Hill	(der) Hügel	huegayl
Hurricane	(der) Orkan	orkaan
Ice	(das) Eis	aais
Island	(die) Insel	inzayl
Lake	(der) See	zay
Leaf	(das) Blatt	blaat
Lightning	(der) Blitz	blits
Marsh	(der) Sumpf	zumpf
Meadow	(die) Wiese	veezay
Mist	(der) Nebel	naybayl
Moon	(der) Mond	mont
Mountain	(der) Berg	bayrg
Ocean	(der) Ozean	otsiaan
Outerspace	(der) Weltraum	veltraaum
Pig	(das) Schwein	shvaain
Planet	(der) Planet	plaanet
Plant	(die) Pflanze	pflaantsay

Pond	(der) Teich	taaish
Rain	(der) Regen	raygen
Rainbow	(der) Regenbogen	raygenbogen
River	(der) Fluss	flus
Root	(die) Wurzel	vurtsayl
Sand	(der) Sand	zaant
Shore	(das) Ufer	oofayr
Shower	(der) Schauer	shaauayr
Shrub	(der) Strauch	shtraaukh
Sky	(der) Himmel	himayl
Snow	(der) Schnee	shnee
Snowdrift	(die) Schneewehe	shneevayhay
Snow storm	(der) Schneesturm	shneesturm
Solar system	(das) Sonnensystem	zonaynziustem
Stalk	(der) Stiel	steel
Star	(der) Stern	shtern
Stone	(der) Stein	shtaain
Stream	(der) Bach	baakh
Sun	(die) Sonne	zonay
Thorn	(der) Dorn	dorn
Thunder	(der) Donner	donayr
Tides	(die) Gezeiten	gaytsaaitayn
Tree	(der) Baum	baaum

Universe	(das) Universum	ooniversoom
Valley	(das) Tal	taal
Vegetation	(die) Vegetation	vaygetatsion
Volcano	(der) Vulkan	fulkaan
Water	(das) Wasser	vaasayr
Waterfall	(der) Wasserfall	vaasayrfaal
Wave	(die) Welle	vaylay
Weather	(das) Wetter	veter
Wind	(der) Wind	vint
World	(die) Welt	velt

Chapter 8

Leisure

Freizeit:-
fraaitsaait

English	German	Pronunciation
Applause	(der) Applaus	aplaaus
Ballet	(das) Ballett	balay
Billiards	(das) Billard	bilaard
Card game	(das) Kartenspiel	kaartaynshpeel
Cartoon	(der) Trickfilm	trikfilm
Chess	(das) Schach	shaakh
Classical music	(die) klassische Musik	klaasishay muzik
Comedy	(die) Komödie	komoedee
Computer game	(das) Computerspiel	computershpeel
Concert	(das) Konzert	kontsert
Contest	(der) Wettbewerb	vetbewerb
Cricket	(das) Kricket	cricket
Crossword	(das) Kreuzworträtsel	kreutsvort-raetsayl
Draw/tie	(das) Unentschieden	oonayntsh-eedayn

Dress rehearsal	(die) Generalprobe	gaynayr-aalprobay
Drum	(die) Trompete	trompete
Entertainment	(die) Unterhaltung	oontayrhaaltung
Exhibition	(die) Ausstellung	aausstelung
Fan	(der) Fan	fan (as in English)
Favourite film	(der) Lieblingsfilm	leeblingsfilm
Film	(der) Film	film (as in English)
Flute	(die) Flöte	floetay
Folkmusic	(die) Volksmusik	folkmuzik (l will be pronounced)
Football	(der) Fußball	fusball
Game	(das) Spiel	shpeel
Game show	(die) Spielshow	shpeelshow
Goal	(das) Tor	tor
Golf	(das) Golf	golf (as in English)
Guitar	(die) Gitarre	gitaaray
Gymnastics	(die) Gymnastik	giumnaastik
Hobby	(das) Hobby	hobby (as in English)
Horror film	(der) Horrorfilm	horrorfilm (as in English)
Instrument	(das) Instrument	instrument (as in English)

Interesting	interessant *(adj.)*	intayraysaant
King of clubs	(der) Kreuz-König	kreuts-koenig
Leisure	(die) Freizeit	fraaitsaait
Literature	(die) Literatur	litaraatuar
Magazine	(die) Zeitschrift	tsaaitshrift
Mountaineering	(das) Bergsteigen	bayrgshtaaigayn
Music	(die) Musik	muzik
Newspaper	(die) Zeitung	tsaaitung
Novel	(der) Roman	romaan
Opera	(die) Oper	opayr
Orchestra	(das) Orchester	orkaystayr
Performance	(die) Vorstellung	forstaylung
Piano	(das) Klavier	klaavear
Picture	(das) Gemälde	gaymaelday
Poem	(das) Gedicht	gaydikht
Poetry	(die) Poesie	poezee
Pop group	(die) Popgruppe	popgrupay
Pop music	(die) Popmusik	popmuzik
Portrait	(das) Porträt	portraet
Racket	(der) Schläger	shlaegayr
Radio station	(der) Radiosender	raadiozayndayr
Saxaphone	(das) Saxofon	zayxofon
Score	(der) Spielstand	shpeelstaand

Sculpture	(die) Skulptur	skulptooar (t will be pronounced)
Song	(das) Lied	leet
Sport	(der) Sport	sport (as in English)
Stage	(die) Bühne	buehnay
Stage play	(das) Theaterstück	theaatayrshtuek
Story	(die) Geschichte	gayshishtay
Swimming	(das) Schwimmen	shvimayn
Table tennis	(das) Tischtennis	tishtenis
Team	(die) Mannschaft	maanshaaft
Tennis	(das) Tennis	tenis (as in English)
Thriller	(der) Thriller	thriller (as in English)
Titel	(der) Titel	titayl
Tournament	(das) Turnier	turnear
Tragedy	(die) Tragödie	traagoedee
TV Channel	(der) Kanal	kanaal
TV serial	(die) Serie	zayree
Violin	(die) Geige	gaaigay
Western	(der) Western	vestayrn

Chapter 9

Education

Ausbildung:-

English	German	Pronunciation
Accurate	genau (*adj.*)	gaynaao
Attention	aufmerksam (*adj.)*	aaufmerkzaam
Biology	(die) Biologie	beeologee
Blackbord	(die) Wandtafel	vaanttaafayl
Boring	langweilig (*adj.*)	laangvaailig
Calculator (pocket)	(der) Taschenrechner	taashayn-rayshnayr
Certificate	(das) Zeugnis	tseugnis
Chalk	(die) Kreide	kraaiday
Chemistry	(die) Chemie	shaymee
Classroom	(das) Klassenzimmer	klaasayntsimar
Comma	(das) Komma	comma (as in English)
Complicated	kompliziert (*adj.*)	komplitseart
Computer	(der) Computer	computer (as in English)
Correct	richtig (*adj.*)	rishtig
Correspondence course	(der) Fernkurs	fernkurs

Creative	kreativ (*adj.*)	kriaativ
Degree	(der) Hochschulabschluss	hokhshulabshlus
Dictation	(das) Diktat	diktaat
Dictionary	(das) Wörterbuch	voertayrbukh
Difficult	schwer (*adj.*)	shwayr
Disobedient	ungehorsam (*adj.*)	oongayhorzaam
Economics	(die) Wirtschaftswissen-schaft	virtsshaafts-visayshaaft
Educated	gebildet (*adj.*)	gebildet
Education	(die) Ausbildung	aausbildung
Entrance exam	(die)Aufnahmeprüfung	aaufnaahmay-pruefung
Eraser	(der) Radiergummi	raadeargoomi
Essay	(der) Aufsatz	aaufzaats
Exam	(die) Prüfung	pruefung
Exam result	(das) Prüfungsergebnis	pruefungs-ergaybnis
Example	(das) Beispiel	baaishpiel
Exercise	(die) Übung	uebung
Exercise book	(das) Heft	hayft
False	falsch (*adj.*)	faalsh
Foreign language	(die) Fremdsprache	fremdshpraakhay
Geography	(die) Erdkunde	erdkunday
Gifted	begabt (*adj.*)	baygaabt

Grade	(die) Note	note
Grammar	(die) Grammatik	gramaatik
Hard-working	fleißig (*adj.*)	flaaisish
Headmaster	(der) Direktor	dirayktor
History	(die) Geschichte	geshishtay
Homework	(die) Hausaufgabe	haausaufgaabay
Hour	(die) Stunde	shtunday
Inaccurate	ungenau (*adj.*)	oongaynaau
Inattentive	unaufmerksam (*adj.*)	onaaufmayrkzaam
Lazy	faul (*adj.*)	faaol
Lecturer	(der) Dozent	dotsaynt
Lunch break	(die) Mittagspause	mitaakspaauzay
Mathematics	(die) Mathematik	maathaymaatik
Mistake	(der) Fehler	fehler
Nursery school	(der) Kindergarten	kindayrgaartayn
Obedient	gehorsam (*adj.*)	gehorzaam
Page	(die) Seite	zaaitay
Paragraph	(der) Absatz	abzaats
Pen	(der) Kugelschreiber	kugaylshraaibayr
Pencil	(der) Bleistift	blaaishtift
Philosophy	(die) Philosophie	philozofee
Phrase	(die) Phrase	fraazay
Physics	(die) Physik	fiuzik
Point	(der) Punkt	punkt

Psychology	(die) Psychologie	psiukologie
Punctuation	(die) Zeichensetzung	saaishaynzetsung
Pupil	(der) Schüler	shuelayr
Qualification	(die) Qualifikation	qvaalifikaatsion
Question	(die) Frage	fraagay
Reply	(die) Antwort	antvort
Research	(die) Forschung	forshung
Ruler	(das) Lineal	liniaal
School	(die) Schule	shulay
Science	(die) Wissenschaft	vissenshaaft
Sentence	(der) Satz	zaats
simple	einfach (*adj.*)	aainfaakh
Sociology	(die) Soziologie	zotsiologee
Solution	(die) Lösung	loezung
Sports ground	(der) Sportplatz	sportplaats
Student (female)	(die) Studentin	studentin
Student (male)	(der) Student	student (as in English)
Study	(das) Studium	shtudioom
Subject	(das) Fach	faakh
Syllabus	(der) Lehrplan	lehrplaan
Teacher (male)	(der) Lehrer	lehrer
Textbook	(das)Lehrbuch	lehrbukh
Theme	(das)Thema	themaa

Theology	(die) Theologie	thiologee
Timetable	(der) Stundenplan	shtundaynplaan
University	(die) Universität	ooniverzitaet
Upbringing	(die) Erziehung	ertseehung

Chapter 10

People

Leute:-
loitay

English	German	Pronunciation
Address	(die) Adresse	adresay
Age	(das) Alter	aalter
Ambitious	ehrgeizig (*adj.*)	ehrgaaitsik
Ancestor	(der) Vorfahr	forfaar
Architect	(der) Architekt	aarshitekt
Aunt	(die) Tante	taantay
Baby	(das) Baby	baby (as in English)
Beautiful	schön (*adj.*)	shoen
Birth	(die) Geburt	gayburt
Bookkeeper	(der) Buchhalter	bukhhaaltayr
Boy	(der) Junge	yungay
Brother	(der) Bruder	brudayr
Builder	(der) Bauarbeiter	baauaarbaaitayr
Bus driver	(der) Busfahrer	busfaahrayr
Child	(das) Kind	kint
Childhood	(die) Kindheit	kinthaait
Cruel	grausam (*adj.*)	graauzaam

Date of birth	(das) Geburtsdatum	gayburtsdaatum
Daughter	(die) Tochter	tokhtar
Daughter in Law	(die) Schwiegertochter	shveegayrtokhtayr
Death	(der) Tod	tod
Depressed	deprimiert (*adj.*)	deprimeart
Divorced	geschieden (*adj.*)	gaysheedayn
Doctor	(der) Arzt	aartst
Engaged	verlobt (*adj.*)	ferlobt
Evil	böse (*adj.*)	boezay
Family	(die) Familie	faamilee
Famous	berühmt (*adj.*)	bayruemt
Farmer	(der) Bauer	baauayr
Father	(der) Vater	faatar
Father-in-law	(der) Schwiegervater	shveegayrfaatar
First name	(der) Vorname	fornaamay
Friend	(der) Freund	froend
Friend(F)/girlfriend	(die) Freundin	froendin
Friendly	freundlich (*adj.*)	freondlish
Funeral/burial	(die) Beerdigung	bayerdung
Funny	lustig (*adj.*)	lustig
Generous	großzügig (*adj.*)	grostsuegig
Girl	(das) Mädchen	maedshayn
Grandchild	(der) Enkel	enkayl
Granddaughter	(die) Enkelin	enkelin
Grandfather	(der) Großvater	grosfaatar

Grandmother	(die) Großmutter	grosmutar
Grandparents	(die) Großeltern	groseltarn
Greedy	gierig (*adj.*)	giarig
Happy	glücklich (*adj.*)	glueklish
Honest	ehrlich (*adj.*)	ehrlish
Housewife	(die) Hausfrau	haausfraau
Husband/man	(der) Mann	maan
Jealous	eifersüchtig *adj*	aaifayrzuekhtik
Lady	(die) Dame	daamay
Lazy	faul (*adj.*)	faaol
Librarian	(der) Bibliothekar	bibliothaykayr
Life	(das) Leben	laybayn
Malicious	boshaft (*adj.*)	boshaaft
Marriage	(die) Hochzeit	hokhtsaait
Married	verheiratet (*adj.*)	fayrhaairaatayt
Matrimony	(die) Ehe	ehay
Modest	bescheiden (*adj.*)	beshaaidayn
Mother	(die) Mutter	mutar
Mother-in-law	(die) Schwiegermutter	shveegayrmutar
Nice	nett (*adj.*)	net
Old	alt (*adj.*)	aalt
Parents	(die) Eltern	eltayrn
Person	(die) Person	perzon
Poor	arm (*adj.*)	aarm
Postman	(der) Briefträger	breeftraegayr

Profession	(der) Beruf	bayroof
Proud	stolz (*adj.*)	shtolts
Rich	reich (*adj.*)	raaish
Sister	(die) Schwester	shvestayr
Son	(der) Sohn	zohn
Son-in-law	(der) Schwiegersohn	shveegayrzon
Stepdaughter	(die) Stieftochter	shteeftokhtar
Stepfather	(der) Stiefvater	shteeffaatar
Stepmother	(die) Stiefmutter	shteefmutar
Stepson	(der) Stiefsohn	shteefzon
Strong	stark (*adj.*)	shtaark
Surname	(der) Nachname	naakhnaamay
Telephonenumber	(die) Telefonnummer	telefon-noomayr
Twin	(der) Zwilling	tsviling
Ugly	hässlich (*adj.*)	haeslish
Uncle	(der) Onkel	onkal
Unhappy	traurig (*adj.*)	traaurig
Widower	(der) Witwer	vitvayr
Window	(die) Witwe	vitvay
Wise	weise (*adj.*)	vaaizay
Woman/wife	(die) Frau	fraau
Young	jung (*adj.*)	yung

Chapter 11

Society

Gesellschaft:-
gezelshaaft

English	German	Pronunciation
Air force	(die) Luftwaffe	luftvaafay
Attack	(der) Angriff	angrif
Bomb	(die) Bombe	bombe
Buddhism	(der) Buddhismus	budhismoos
Buddhist (male)	(der) Buddhist	buddhist
Ceremony	(die) Zeremonie	tseremonee
Christian (male)	(der) Christ	krist
Christianity	(das) Christentum	kristayntum
Civilized	zivilisiert (*adj.*)	tsivilizeart
Community	(die) Gemeinschaft	gaymaainshaaft
Conquest	(die) Eroberung	erobayrung
Corruption	(die) Korruption	korrupsioan
Criminal act	(das) Verbrechen	fayrbraykhayn
Culture	(die) Kultur	kooltuar
Dangerous	gefährlich (*adj.*)	gayfaehrlish
Death penalty	(die) Todesstrafe	todaysstraafay
Deception	(der) Betrug	betrug

Democracy	(die) Demokratie	demokratee
Demonstration	(die) Demonstration	daymons-traatsion
Dictatorship	(die) Diktatur	diktaatuar
Economy	(die) Wirtschaft	virtshaaft
Election	(die) Wahl	vaal
Extortion	(die) Erpressung	expresung
Factory	(die) Fabrik	faabreek
Fair	gerecht (*adj.*)	gayraykht
Faith	(der) Glaube	glaaubay
Freedom	(die) Freiheit	fraaihaait
Government	(die) Regierung	raygierung
Guilty	schuldig (*adj.*)	shuldig
Hindu	(der) Hindu	hindu
Holy	heilig *adj.*	haailig
Independence	(die) Unabhängigkeit	oonabhaengish-kaait
Industry	(die) Industrie	industree
Interest rate	(der) Zinssatz	tsinszaats
Islam	(der) Islam	islaam
Jew	(der) Jude	yuday
Judaism	(der) Judaismus	yudaaismus
King	(der) König	koenig
Law	(das) Gesetz	gayzayts

Majority	(die) Mehrheit	mearhaait
Minority	(die) Minderheit	mindayrhaait
Modern	modern (*adj.*)	modern
Murder	(der) Mord	mord
Navy	(die) Marine	maarinay
Opinion poll	(die) Meinungsumfrage	maainungs-fraagay
Opression	(die) Unterdrückung	oontardruekung
Party	(die) Partei	paartaai
Peace	(der) Frieden	freedayn
Police	(die) Polizei	politsaai
Policy	(die) Politik	politeek
Political	politisch (*adj.*)	politish
Population	(die) Bevölkerung	befoelkayrung
powerful	mächtig (*adj.*)	maeshtig
Prayer	(das) Gebet	gaybayt
President	(der) Präsident	praezidaynt
Prison	(das) Gefängnis	gayfaengnis
Public	öffentlich (*adj.*)	oefentlish
Queen	(die) Königin	koenigin
Rape	(die) Vergewaltigung	fayrvaaltigung
Religion	(die) Religion	rayligioon
Rifle	(das) Gewehr	gevayr
Right	(das) Recht	resht

Robbery	(der) Raub	raaub
Society	(die) Gesellschaft	gayzayshaaft
Statement	(die) Aussage	aauszaagay
Terrorism	(der) Terrorismus	terorismoos
Theft	(der) Diebstahl	deebshtaal
Trade	(der) Handel	haandayl
Tradition	(die) Tradition	traaditsion
Tradition	(der) Brauch	braaukh
Treason	(der) Verrat	fayrraat
Treaty	(der) Vertrag	fayrtraag
Trial	(der) Prozess	protsays
Unemployment	(die) Arbeitslosigkeit	aarbaaitlosigkaait
War	(der) Krieg	kreeg
Weapon	(die) Waffe	vaafay
Witness	(der) Zeuge	tseugay

Chapter 12

Town

Stadt:-
shtat

English	German	Pronunciation
Art gallery	(die) Galerie	gaalayree
Bank	(die) Bank	baank
Bench	(die) Bank	baank
Bookshop	(die) Buchhandlung	bukhhaandlung
Bridge	(die) Brücke	bruekay
Building	(das) Gebäude	gaybaeuday
Building site	(die) Baustelle	baaostaylay
Cafe	(das) Café	kayfe
Cake shop	(die) Konditorei	konditoraayee
Car park	(der) Parkplatz	paarkplaats
Cash	(das) Bargeld	baargeld
Cash machine	(der) Geldautomat	geldaautomaat
Cathedral	(der) Dom	dom
Changing room	(die) Umkleidekabine	umklaaidkaabinay
Cheap	billig (*adj.*)	beelik
Cheque	(der) Scheck	shek

Church	(die) Kirche	kirshay
Cinema	(das) Kino	keeno
Circus	(der) Zirkus	tsirkus
Coin	(die) Münze	muentsay
Corner	(die) Ecke	eckay
Counter	(der) Schalter	shaaltayr
Credit card	(die) Kreditkarte	kreditkaartay
Crossing	(der) Überweg	uebayrveg
Crossroad	(die) Kreuzung	kreutsung
Customer	(der) Kunde	koonday
Department store	(das) Kaufhaus	kaaufhaaus
Entrance	(der) Eingang	aaingaang
Escalator	(die) Rolltreppe	roltrepe
Exit	(der) Ausgang	aaoosgaang
Expensive	teuer (*adj.*)	teuayr
Fence	(der) Zaun	tsaaun
Fire station	(die) Feuerwache	feuervaakhay
Fountain	(der) Brunnen	brunayn
Gift	(das) Geschenk	geshaynk
Grocery shop	(das) Lebensmittel-geschäft	laybaynsmitayl-gayshaeft
Hospital	(das) Krankenhaus	kraankaynhouse
Impressive	beeindruckend (*adj.*)	bayaaind-rookaynd

Kiosk	(der) Kiosk	kiosk
Law court	(der) Gerichtshof	gayrishtshof
Leisure centre	(das) Freizeitzentrum	fraaitsaaitt-sayntrum
Library	(die) Bücherei	bueshayrai
Lift	(der) Aufzug	aaooftsug
Lost property	(die) Fundsachen	foondzaakhan
Magnificent	großartig (*adj.*)	grosaartik
Main street	(die) Hauptstraße	haauptstraasay
Market	(der) Markt	maarkt
Money	(das) Geld	gayld
Monument	(das) Denkmal	denkmaal
Mosque	(die) Moschee	moshee
Museum	(das) Museum	muziom
Office	(das) Büro	buero
Park	(der) Park	paark
Pavement	(der) Bürgersteig	buergayrshtaaik
Police station	(die) Polizeiwache	politsaaivaakhay
Post box	(der) Briefkasten	breefkaastayn
Post office	(die) Post	post
Refund	(die) Rückerstattung	ruekerstaatung
Restaurant	(das) Restaurant	restaurant (as in English)

Road sign	(das) Verkehrszeichen	fayhrskayhrt-saaishayn
Road/street	(die) Straße	straasay
Second-hand	gebraucht (*adj.*)	gaybraaukht
Shop	(das) Geschäft	gayshaeft
Shopping centre	(das) Einkaufszentrum	aainkaaufst-sayntrum
Special offer	(das) Sonderangebot	zondayrn-angaybot
Stadium	(das) Stadion	shtaadion
Subway	(die) Unterführung	oontayrfuehrung
Supermarket	(der) Supermarkt	zupayrmaarkt
Swimming pool	(das) Schwimmbad	shwimbaad
Telephone booth	(die) Telefonzelle	telefontsyallay
Theatre	(das) Theater	thayaatayr
Tower	(der) Turm	toorm
Town hall	(das) Rathaus	raathaus
Traffic	(der)Verkehr	fayrkayhr
Traffic lights	(die) Ampel	aampayl
Tunnel	(der) Tunnel	toonayl
Zoo	(der) Zoo	tsoo

Chapter 13

Travel

Reise:-
raaizay

English	German	Pronunciation
Aeroplane	(das) Flugzeug	flugtseug
Africa	(das) Afrika	africa (as in English)
Airport	(der) Flughafen	flughaafayn
Antarctic Ocean	(das) Südpolarmeer	zuedpolarmayr
Arctic Ocean	(das) Nordpolarmeer	nordpolarmayr
Asia	(das) Asien	aazeeayn
Atlantic Ocean	(der) Atlantische	atlaantishay
Australia	(das) Australien	aaustraaliayn
Austria	(das) Österreich	oestayraaish
Baltic Sea	(die) Ostsee	ostzay
Beach	(der) Strand	shtraand
Belgium	(das) Belgien	belgeeayn
Bicycle	(das) Fahrrad	faahrraad
Black Sea	(das) Schwarze Meer	shvaartsay mayr
Border	(die) Grenze	grayntsay
Brazil	(das) Brasilien	braazileeayn

British	britisch (*adj.*)	british (as in English)
Bus	(der) Bus	boos
Bus stop	(die) Bushaltestelle	booshaalt-shtaylay
Canada	(das) Kanada	canada (as in English)
Car	(das) Auto	aauto
China	(das) China	shinaa
Customs/duty	(der) Zoll	tsoll
Danish	dänisch (*adj.*)	denish
Denmark	(das) Dänemark	denmark
Direction	(die) Richtung	rishtung
District	(das) Gebiet	gaybeet
East	(der) Osten	ostayn
Egypt	(das) Ägypten	aegiuptayn
England	(das) England	englaand
English	englisch (*adj.*)	aynglish
Equator	(der) Äquator	equator (as in English)
Europe	(das) Europa	oyeropaa
Excursion	(der) Ausflug	aausflug
Exotic	exotisch (*adj.*)	exotish
Foreign	fremd (*adj.*)	fremt

Foreign currency	(die) Devisen	dayvizayn
Foreigner	(der) Ausländer	aauslaendayr
France	(das) Frankreich	fraankraaish
French	französisch (*adj.*)	frantsoezish
German	deutsch (*adj.*)	doiach
Germany	(das) Deutschland	doiachlaand
Greece	(das) Griechenland	greeshaynlaand
Holland	(das) Holland	holaand
Hotel	(das) Hotel	hotayl
Hungarian	ungarisch (*adj.*)	oongaarish
Hungary	(das) Ungarn	oongaarn
India	(das) Indien	indiayn
Indian	indisch (*adj.*)	indish
Indian Ocean	(der) Indische Ozean	indishay otsiaan
Ireland	(das) Irland	irlaand
Italy	(das) Italien	itaaliayn
Japan	(das) Japan	yapaan
Japanese	japanisch (*adj.*)	yapaanish
Journey	(die) Reise	raaizay
Land/country	(das) Land	laand
Language	(die) Sprache	spraakhay
Light	leicht (*adj.*)	laaisht
Luggage	(das) Gepäck	gaypaek
Mediterranean Sea	(das) Mittelmeer	mitaylmayr

Mexico	(das) Mexiko	mexico (as in English)
Motorcycle	(das) Motorrad	motorraad
Motorway	(die) Autobahn	autobaan
Netherlands	(die) Niederlande	nidayrlaande
New Zealand	(das) Neuseeland	noizaylaand
Norden	(der) Norden	nordayn
North America	(das) Nordamerika	nordaamayrikaa
North Pole	(der) Nordpol	nordpol
North Sea	(die) Nordsee	nordzay
Norway	(das) Norwegen	norwaygayn
Pacific Ocean	(der) Pazifische Ozean	paatsifishay-otsiaan
Passport	(der) Pass	paas
Petrol	(das) Benzin	bentsin
Petrol station	(die) Tankstelle	taankshtaylay
Poland	(das) Polen	polayn
Port	(der) Hafen	haafayn
Postcard	(die) Postkarte	postkaartay
Pourtgal	(das) Portugal	portugaal
Railway	(die) Eisenbahn	aaizaynbaan
Railway station	(der) Bahnhof	baanhof
Rucksack	(der) Rucksack	ruckzaak
Russia	(das) Russland	ruslaand

Russian	russisch (*adj.*)	rusish
Scooter	(der) Roller	rolayr
Scotland	(das) Schottland	shotlaand
Scottish	schottisch (*adj.*)	scottish (as in English)
Seasick	seekrank (*adj.*)	zaykraank
Ship	(das) Schiff	shif
Slow	langsam (*adj.*)	laangzaam
South	(der) Süden	zuedayn
South America	(das) Südamerika	zuedaamayrikaa
South Pole	(der) Südpol	zuedpol
Spain	(das) Spanien	spaanien
Spanish	spanisch (*adj.*)	spaanish
Street map	(der) Stadtplan	shtatplaan
Suitcase	(der) Koffer	kofayr
Sweden	(das) Schweden	shvaydayn
Swedish	schwedisch (*adj.*)	shvaydish
Switzerland	(die) Schweiz	shvaaits
Taxi	(das) Taxi	taaxi
Tent	(das) Zelt	tselt
Tour	(die) Tour	tooar
Tourism	(der) Tourismus	tourismoos
Town/city	(die) Stadt	shtat
Train	(der) Zug	tsug

Tram	(die) Straßenbahn	shtraasaynbaan
Tropical	tropisch (*adj.*)	tropish
Turkey	(die) Türkei	tuerkaai
Turkish	türkisch (*adj.*)	tuerkish
United States	(die) Vereinigten Staaten	fayraaiaynigtayn-staatayn
Village	(das) Dorf	dorf
Visa	(das) Visum	vizum
West	(der) Westen	vestayn
World	(die) Welt	velt
Youth hostel	(die) Jugendherberge	yugenthayr-bayrgay

Chapter 14

Number

Zahl:-
tsaal

Number	English	German	Pronunciation
0	zero	null	nool
1	one	eins	aains
2	two	zwei	tswaai
3	three	drei	draai
4	four	vier	fear
5	five	fünf	fuenf
6	six	sechs	zaykhs
7	seven	sieben	zeebayn
8	eight	acht	aakht
9	nine	neun	noyn
10	ten	zehn	tsayn
11	eleven	elf	elf
12	twelve	zwölf	tswoelf
13	thirteen	dreizehn	draaitsayn
14	fourteen	vierzehn	feartsayn
15	fifteen	fünfzehn	fuenftsayn

16	sixteen	sechzehn	zaykhtsayn
17	seventeen	siebzehn	zeebtsayn
18	eighteen	achtzehn	aakhtsayn
19	nineteen	neunzehn	noyntsayn
20	twenty	zwanzig	tswantsig
21	twenty-one	einundzwanzig	aainunttsvaantsig
22	twenty-two	zweiundzwanzig	tswaaiunttsvaantsig
23	twenty-three	dreiundzwanzig	draaiunttsvaantsig
24	twenty-four	vierundzwanzig	fearunttsvaantsig
25	twenty-five	fünfundzwanzig	fuenfunttsvaantsig
26	twenty-six	sechsundzwanzig	zaykhunttsvaantsig
27	twenty-seven	siebenundzwanzig	zeebaynunttsvantsig
28	twenty-eight	achtundzwanzig	aakhtunttsvaantsig
29	twenty-nine	neunundzwanzig	noynunttsvaantsig
30	thirty	dreißig	draaisig
31	thirty-one	einunddreißig	aainuntdraaisig
32	thirty-two	zweiunddreißig	tswaaiuntdraaisig
33	thirty-three	dreiunddreißig	draaiuntdraaisig
34	thirty-four	vierunddreißig	fearuntdraaisig
35	thirty-five	fünfunddreißig	fuenfuntdraaisig
36	thirty-six	sechsunddreißig	zaykhsuntdraaisig
37	thirty-seven	siebenunddreißig	zeebaynuntdraaisig
38	thirty-eight	achtunddreißig	aakhtuntdraaisig
39	thirty-nine	neununddreißig	noynuntdraaisig

40	fourty	vierzig	feartsig
41	fourty-one	einundvierzig	aainuntfeartsig
42	fourty-two	zweiundvierzig	tswaaiuntfeartsig
43	fourty-three	dreiundvierzig	draaiuntfeartsig
44	fourty-four	vierundvierzig	fearuntfeartsig
45	fourty-five	fünfundvierzig	fuenfuntfeartsig
46	fourty-six	sechsundvierzig	zaykhsuntfeartsig
47	fourty-seven	siebenundvierzig	zeebaynuntfeartsig
48	fourty-eight	achtundvierzig	aakhtuntfeartsig
49	fourty-nine	neunundvierzig	noynuntfeartsig
50	fifty	fünfzig	fuenftsig
51	fifty-one	einundfünfzig	aainuntfuenftsig
52	fifty-two	zweiundfünfzig	tsvaaiuntfuenftsig
53	fifty-three	dreiundfünfzig	draaiuntfuenftsig
54	fifty-four	vierundfünfzig	fearuntfuenftsig
55	fifty-five	fünfundfünfzig	fuenfuntfuenftsig
56	fifty-six	sechsundfünfzig	zekhsuntfuenftsig
57	fifty-seven	siebenundfünfzig	zeebaynuntfuenftsig
58	fifty-eight	achtundfünfzig	aakhtuntfuenftsig
59	fifty-nine	neunundfünfzig	noynuntfuenftsig
60	sixty	sechzig	zekhstsig
61	sixty-one	einundsechzig	aainuntzekhstig
62	sixty-two	zweiundsechzig	tsvaaiuntzekhstsig
63	sixty-three	dreiundsechzig	draaiuntzekhstsig

64	sixty-four	vierundsechzig	fearuntzekhstsig
65	sixty-five	fünfundsechzig	fuenfuntzaekhstsig
66	sixty-six	sechsundsechsig	zaykhsuntzaekhstsig
67	sixty-seven	siebenundsechsig	zeebaynuntzaekhstsig
68	sixty-eight	achtundsechsig	aakhtuntzaekhstsig
69	sixty-nine	neunundsechsig	noynuntzekhstsig
70	seventy	siebzig	zeebtsig
71	seventy-one	einundsiebzig	aainuntzeebtsig
72	seventy-two	zweiundsiebzig	tsvaaiuntzeebtsig
73	seventy-three	dreiundsiebzig	draaiuntzeebtsig
74	seventy-four	vierundsiebzig	fearuntzeebtsig
75	seventy-five	fünfundsiebzig	fuenfuntzeebtsig
76	seventy-eight	achtundsiebzig	zaykhsuntzeebtsig
77	seventy-seven	siebenundsiebzig	zeebaynuntzeebtsig
78	seventy-eight	achtundsiebzig	aakhtuntzeebtsig
79	seventy-nine	neunundsiebzig	noynuntzeebtsig
80	eighty	achtzig	aakhttsig
81	eighty-one	einundachtzig	aainuntaakhtsig
82	eighty-two	zweiundachtzig	tsvaaiuntaakhtsig
83	eighty-three	dreiundachtzig	draaiuntaakhtsig
84	eighty-four	vierundachtzig	fearuntaakhtsig
85	eighty-five	fünfundachtzig	fuenuntfaakhtsig
86	eighty-six	sechsundachtzig	zaykhsuntaakhtsig
87	eighty-seven	siebenundachtzig	zeebaynuntaakhtsig

88	eighty-eight	achtundachtzig	aakhtuntaakhtsig
89	eighty-nine	neunundachtzig	noynuntaakhtsig
90	ninety	neunzig	noyntsig
91	ninety-two	einundneunzig	aainuntnoyntsig
92	ninety-two	zweiundneunzig	tswaaiuntnoyntsig
93	ninety-three	dreiundneunzig	draaiuntnoyntsig
94	ninety-four	vierundneunzig	fearuntnoyntsig
95	ninety-five	fünfundneunzig	fuenfuntnoyntsig
96	ninety-six	sechsundneunzig	zaykhsuntnoyntsig
97	ninety-seven	siebenundneunzig	zeebaynuntnoyntsig
98	ninety-eight	achtundneunzig	aakhtuntnoyntsig
99	ninety-nine	neunundneunzig	noynuntnoyntsig
100	hundred	hundert	hundert
101	One hundred-one	hunderteins	hundertaains
200	two hundred	zweihundert	tsvaaihundert
201	two hundred-one	zweihunderteins	tsvaaihundertaains
1000	thousand	tausend or-eintausend	taauzaynt or-aaintaauzaynt
1001	One thousand-one	tausendeins	taauzayntaains
1,000,000	One million	eine Million	aainay milioon

Rules:

1. For decimal numbers (Dezimalzahlen), German uses a comma (das Komma) where English uses a decimal point: 0.638 (English) = 0,638 (spoken: "null Komma sechs drei acht") or 1.08 (English) = 1,08 (spoken: "eins Komma null acht").
2. One o'clock ein Uhr (time, no ending on 'ein') one/a clock eine Uhr (article, -e ending on 'ein') (date) on the first am ersten on 1 May, on May first, the first of May am ersten Mai, am 1. Mai.
3. Der zweite, der 2. (second) - halb, die Hälfte (half, one-half) Often the alternative form zwo is used to avoid confusion with
4. To say "in the twenties (the '20s)" - short for "the 1920s" - in German you say "in den zwangziger Jahren." The same method is used for all the other decades ('30s, '40s, etc.) except for the 1900s and the teens.
5. Note that, unlike the other tens (20, 40, 50, etc.), dreißig has no 'z' in its spelling.
6. Some mathematics terms Mathematische Ausdrücke add addieren algebra 'e' Algebra calculus 's' Differentialrechnen, 's' Integralrechnen divide dividieren divided by durch ten divided by two zehn durch zwei (10/2) equals ist, gleicht Five and/plus six equals/is eleven. Fünf und sechs ist elf. equation (math) 'e' Gleichung, 'e' Gleichungsformel formula (math) 'e' Formel geometry 'e' Geometrie minus, less minus (MEE-noos), weniger (VENN-eh-guhr) multiply multiplizieren plus, and plus (PLOOS), und two and/plus two zwei und/plus zwei subtract subtrahieren times (2x3 = 6) mal (2 mal 3 = 6) once, one time einmal five times fünfmal trigonometry 'e' Trigonometrie.

7. In German 1000/1,000 is written/printed as either 1000, 1.000 or 1000 - using a decimal point (Punkt) or a space where English uses a comma. This also applies to all German numbers above 1,000. For decimal numbers, German uses a comma (das Komma) where English uses a decimal point: 1.638 (English) = 1,638 (spoken: "eins Komma sechs drei acht").

8. YEARS - JAHRE

   1100 elfhundert (year, number) or tausendeinhundert (number only) For the years 1100 to 1999 in German, you must say the hundert, as for 1152 (elfhundertzweiundfünfzig) or 1864 (achtzehnhundertvierundsechzig). 1200 zwölfhundert (year, number) or tausendzweihundert (number only)

   im Jahre: "Im Jahre 1350..." ("dreizehnhundertfünfzig" - "In the year 1350...") If the word "Jahr" is left out, then the year is used by itself, with no "im" (in the) or "in." Example: "He was born in 1958." = "Er ist im Jahre 1958 geboren." or "Er ist 1958 geboren." Similarly: "Kolumbus hat 1492 Amerika entdeckt." ("vierzehnhundertzweiundneunzig" - "Columbus dicovered America in 1492.").

   1800 achtzehnhundert (year, number)

   1900 neunzehnhundert (year, number)

   2000 zweitausend (year, number; more below)

   AD, BC, BCE/CE: To convey the Christian calendar's use of AD (*anno domini*, "year of our Lord") and BC (before Christ), German uses n.Chr. (nach Christus, AD) and v.Chr. (vor Christus, BC). BCE/CE (Before the/Common Era) was used mostly in East Germany: v.u.Z. (vor unserer Zeitrechnung, BCE/BC) and u.Z. (unserer Zeitrechnung, CE/AD).

"In the year 2001" can be spoken/written in German as "im Jahre 2001" or "im Jahr 2001" ("zweitausendeins"). If the word "Jahr" is left out, then the year is used by itself, with no "im" (in the) or "in." Example: "He was born in (the year) 2001." = "Er ist im Jahre 2001 geboren." or "Er ist 2001 geboren."

9. In German one million is eine Million, but two million is zwei Millionen („two millions").

10. Billion eine Milliarde - der milliardste (the billionth)

    An American billion is a German Milliarde. A German Billion is an American "trillion." trillion eine Billion - der billionste (the trillionth).

Chapter 15

Months

Monate:-
monaatay

English	German	Pronunciation
January	Januar	yaanuaar
February	Februar	februaar
March	März	maerts
April	April	april
May	Mai	maai
June	Juni	yuni
July	Juli	yuli
August	August	augoost
September	September	zeptember
October	Oktober	oktobayr
November	November	november
December	Dezember	daytsaymbayr

Days

Tage:-
taage

English	German	Pronunciation
Sunday	Sonntag	zontaak
Monday	Montag	montaak
Tuesday	Dienstag	deenstaak
Wednesday	Mittwoch	meetvokh
Thursday	Donnerstag	donerstaak
Friday	Freitag	Fraaitaak
Saturday	Samstag	saamstaak
Today	Heute	hoytay
Tomorrow	Morgen	morgayn
Yesterday	Gestern	gestern

Season

Die Jahreszeit:-
dee yaarestsaait

English	German	Pronunciation
Autumn	Herbst	hayrbst
Spring	Frühling	fruehling
Summer	Sommer	zomayr
Winter	Winter	vinter

Part-III
Chapter 1

Related German and English Words

Some of the most common German words, often repeated in everyday speech, closely resemble English words of the same meaning. The pronunciation differs, of course, but this will offer few difficulties.

(a) **Some common nouns:** All nouns are capitalized in German.

English	German	Pronunciation
Man	Mann	maan
Grass	Gras	graas
Ball	Ball	ball
Park	Park	paark
Hand	Hand	haant
Hat	Hut	hoot

(b) **Some frequently used adjectives:**

English	German	Pronunciation
Warm	warm	vaarm
Cold	kalt	kaalt
Old	alt	aalt
New	neu	noy
Good	gut	gut

Blue	blau	blaau
Brown	braun	braaun
Long	lang	laang
Full	voll	fol
Round	rund	runt

(c) **Some freuently used verbs:** The infinitive of these German verbs ends in –en or –n. If these endings are removed from the following verbs, remarkable resemblence to English verbs of the same meaning, will be seen.

English	German	Pronunciation
To sing	singen	zingayn
To spring	springen	springayn
To bring	bringen	bringayn
To see	sehen	zayhayn
To help	helfen	helfen
To come	kommen	komen
To fall	fallen	falen
To send	senden	zayndayn
To begin	beginnen	bayginnen
To wash	washen	vaashayn
To have	haben	haabayn
To bind	binden	bindayn

Chapter 2

Good Wishes

Gute Wünsche:-
gutay vuenshay

(a) Birthday/Geburtstag:-

Best wishes
Alles Gute
alles gutay

Congratulations
Herzlichen Glückwunsch
hertslish glueckwunsh

Congratulations
Ich gratuliere
ikh graatulieray

Happy Birthday!
Alles Gute zum Geburtstag!
alays gutay tsum Geboortstaak

Many happy returns of the day!
Viel Glück zum Geburtstag!
feel glueck tsum geboortstaak

German Happy Birthday Song (Traditional)

Long may he live! Long may he live!
Hoch soll er leben! Hoch soll er leben!
hokh zol er leben! Hokh zol zee leben!

Long may she live! Long may she live!
Hoch soll sie leben! Hoch soll sie leben!
Dreimal hoch! (Three cheers!)

hokh zoll zee leben! hokh zoll zee leben!
draaimal hokh!

Note: This brief song also serves as the German equivalent of "For He's a Jolly Good Fellow." The tune is different from that of "Happy Birthday" in English, which is actually heard more often at German birthday parties than "Hoch soll er leben!

(b) General/Allgemeines:-

A blessing in disguise.
Glück im Unglück.
glueck im ungluek

Enjoy your meal!
Mahlzeit! Guten Appetit!
maaltsaait/gutayn aapetit

Have a good trip!
Gute Reise!
gutay raaizay

Good luck!
Viel Glück!
feel glueck

Lucky fellow
Das Glückskind
das glueckskint

To your health! (toast)
Auf deine/Ihre Gesundheit!
aauf daainay/ihray Gezunthaait

You were lucky.
Da hast du Glück gehabt.
daa haast du glueck gehaabt

I wish you success!
Viel Erfolg!
feel erfolg

(c) Graduation/Schulabschluß:-

Best wishes... Alles Gute...
Congratulations... Herzlichen Glückwunsch...
Congratulations... Ich gratuliere...

On graduating from high school (Germany)
Zum bestandenen Abitur!
tsum bestaandenen Aabituar

On graduating from high school (Austria/Switz.)
Zur bestandenen Matura!
tsooar bestaandenen Maaturaa

On graduating with a master's degree
Der Magister! Zur Sponsion!
dayr maagistayr/tsooar sponzion

On graduating with a doctorate
Die Doktorarbeit! Zur Promotion
dee doktoraarbaait/tsooar promotsion

(d) Marriage & Anniversary
Hochzeit & Jahrestag
hokhtsaait & yaarestaak

Congratulations... Herzlichen Glückwunsch...

On your engagement!
Zur/zu deiner/zu Ihrer Verlobung!
tsooar/tsu daainayr/tsu ihrayr fayrlobung

On your wedding!
Zur/zu deiner/zu Ihrer Hochzeit/
tsooar/tsu daainayr/tsu ihrayr hokhtsaait

On the happy event!
Zum freudigen Ereignis!
tsum freudigayn eraaignis

On your golden/silver wedding anniversary!
Zur goldenen/silbernen Hochzeit!
tsooar goldenen/zilbernen hokhtsaait

Chapter 3

Communication

Kommunikation:-
komunikaatsion

(a) Telephone:-

Many German public phones only accept a telephone card, not coins.

Answer the phone.
Den Hörer abheben/abnehmen, sich melden
dayn hoerayr abheben/abnehmen, zish melden

There was no answer.
Keiner/Niemand hat sich gemeldet.
kaainayr/neemaand hat zish gemeldet

Answering machine
Der Anrufbeantworter
dayr anrufbeantwortayr

Area code, dialing code
Die Vorwahl, die Vorwahlnummer
dee forvaal, die forvaalnumayr

Battery (rechargeable)
Der Akku (in wireless phones)
dayr aaku

The line is busy.
Die Leitung ist besetzt.
dee laaitung ist bezetst

To call
Anrufen, telefonieren
anrufen, telefonearen

Cell phone, mobile phone
Das Handy, das Mobiltelefon
das handy, das mobiltelefon

Insert coins.
Münzen einwerfen/einstecken.
muentsayn aainverfen/einsteken

A good/bad connection
Eine gute/schlechte Verbindung
aainay gutay/shlekhtay ferbindung

Cordless phone
Das schnurlose Telefon
das shnurlozay telefon

Dial direct.
Direkt wählen, durchwählen.
deerekt vaehlen, durshwaehlen

Dial tone
Das Amtszeichen, das Freizeichen.
das aamtstsaaishen, das fraaitsaaishen

Dial the/a wrong number
Die/eine falsche Nummer wählen
dee/aainay faalshay numayr vaehlayn

Sorry, wrong number.
Tut mir leid, falsch verbunden.
toot mear laait, faalsh numayr

(b) E-mail:-

Internet
Das Internet, das Netz

Modem
Das Modem

To check one's email
Die E-Mail abrufen
dee e-mail abrufen

To send an email message
Eine E-Mail senden/schicken
aainay e-mail zenden/shiken

Das E-Mail? Some Germans will say that email in German is *das* rather than *die.* But since the English word stands for die E-Post or die E-Post-Nachricht, it's difficult to justify *das*. Dictionaries say it's die (feminine). (*Das Email* means "enamel.")

(c) Fax:-

To fax
Faxen
faaxayn

Fax machine
Das Faxgerät
das faaxgeraet

One can send a fax from most larger German post offices. You pay for each page sent and any phone charges.

(d) GSM (Global System for Mobile communications)

GSM is a digital mobile phone system used in Germany and most of Europe. Germany has four main competing digital phone standards: D1, D2, E2, and e-plus - all variations of GSM, and none of them compatible with US wireless systems. T-Mobile, Cingular, and some other US wireless firms do use GSM but on a different band than in Europe. A multi-band cell phone is used, that works in the US and Europe.

Key lock
Die Tastensperre (cell phone)
dee taastenspere

Line (phone)
Die Leitung
dee laaitung

Local call
Das Ortsgespräch
das ortsgayspraekh

Long distance call
Das Ferngespräch
das fayrngespraekh

To make a long distance call
Ein Ferngespräch führen
aain fayrngayspraekh fuehrayn

Message
Die Gesprächsnotiz, die Nachricht
dee gayspraekhsnotits, dee naakhrisht

Not a working number. (Your call can't go through.)
Kein Anschluß unter dieser Nummer.
kaain anshlus untayr deezayr noomayr

Pay phone
Das öffentliche Telefon
das oeffayntlishay Telefon

On the phone
Am Apparat/am Telefon
am aparaat/am telefon

Phone card
Die Telefonkarte
dee telefonkaartay

The phone's ringing.
Das Telefon klingelt/läutet.
das telefon klingaylt/laeutayt

Ring
Der Klingelton, der Signalton
dayr klingelton, dayr zignaalton

Signal strength
Die Signalstärke (for cell phone)
dee zignaalstaerkay

SIM card
Die SIM-Karte (Chip used in GMS mobile phones)
dee SIM-kaartay

SMS
Der SMS (Short Message Service)
dayr SMS

Telephone bill
Die Telefonrechnung
dee telefonreshnung

Telephone book/directory
Das Telefonbuch
das telefonbukh

Telephone number
Die Telefonnummer
dee telefonnumayr

T-Mobile is a division of Germany's Deutsche Telekom.

Toll-free
Gebührenfrei, zum Nulltarif
gaybuehraynfraai, tsum nooltaarif

Toll-free numbers in Germany begin with either 0130 (old) or 0800, the new so-called "freecall" prefix. Actually, a trend seen in many magazine ads today is the use of a 180-number with a per-minute rate of 15 euro cents—not really that cheap. Some German dial-around services offer rates of between 5 and 10 euro cents/min.

It is now possible to call 1-800 (and 888/877) toll-free numbers in North America from Europe, but you will be charged the normal long distance rate.

(d) WAP/das WAP (Wireless Application Protocol):-

WAP is a protocol that allows Web pages to be displayed on WAP-capable wireless telephones. Web pages/sites must be specially formatted in order to function on a WAP phone.

Wireless telephone
Das drahtlose Telefon
das draahtlozay telefon

Chapter 4

Personal letter Writing in German

English	*German*	*Pronunciation*
Envelope	*(der) Umschlag*	*oomshlaag*
Title	*(der) Titel*	*titayl*

Mr, Mrs/Ms, Miss These titles are usually not abbreviated in German. German uses Frau for both Mrs and Ms (any woman 18 or older). Herrn - Frau - Fräulein Note the 'n' ending on Herrn, reflecting the understood phrase: an Herrn XYZ (to Mr. XYZ)

Address (female): Mrs (Ms) Maria SchmidtSchillerstrasse 19 (19 Schiller St.)postal code & city (D = Germany, A = Austria, CH = Switz.).

Die Anschrift (weiblich): Frau Maria Schmidt (Fräulein if under 18)Schillerstraße 18D-23451 KleindorfGermany (if writing from outside the country).

Note: Straße is often abbreviated Str. Other types of streets: Allee (avenue, boulevard), Gasse (lane), Weg (way, drive).

Return Address: Sarah Brown253 Fall LaneCactus City, NV 89101USA (if mailed from abroad).

Der Absender: A German return address (preceded by the abbreviation Abs.) usually goes on the back of the envelope.

On the Envelope/ auf dem Umschlag Air Mail Luftpost (Germany) - Flugpost (Austria).

c/o - in care of "John Smith c/o the Jones"

bei "John Smith bei Jones"

P.O. Box 12345Postfach 12345

Registered Mail Eingeschrieben

(postage) stamp die Briefmarke

Salutations/Anreden:

Dear Maria, Liebe Maria *(leebay maariaa)*, (female, e-ending)

Dear Hans, Lieber Hans *(leebar haans)*, (male, er-ending)

Dear Maria and Hans, Liebe Maria, lieber Hans,

Dear Dad/Dear Mom, Lieber Vati, *(leebar fati)*, Liebe Mutti, *(leebay muti)*

Dear Friends, Liebe Freunde,

My Dearest Karl, Mein liebster Karl, (Maain leebstayr Kaarl)

My Dearest Maria, Meine liebste Maria, (Maainay leebstay Maaria)

Address (male): Mr Karl BraunMozartstrasse 35 (35 Mozart St.)postal code & city (A=Austria, D=Germany, CH=Switz.).

Die Anschrift(männlich): Herrn Karl Braun (Note the n!)Mozartstraße 35A-3451 SchöndorfAustria (if writing from outside the country).

Personal Letter: To a Close Friend or Relative

Cactus City, den 25. Nov. 2004

Liebe Maria,

Über deinen letzten Brief haben wir uns sehr gefreut! Tut mir leid, dass ich schon lange nicht geantwortet habe, aber nun endlich bekommst du mal wieder ein Lebenszeichen von uns.

Wie du schon weißt, war Jim drei Wochen lang in Asien auf Geschäftsreise. Da musste ich hier zu Hause fast alles machen und kam nie dazu, dir zu schreiben. Aber mittlerweile läuft fast alles bei uns wieder 'normal' and ich habe ein bisschen Zeit, um zur Feder zu greifen.

Am Mittwoch waren wir bei Barbara und Dan zum Abendessen. Sie lassen auch grüßen und hoffen dich wieder im Sommer in Berlin zu besuchen. Dan arbeitet immer noch bei...

Schöne Grüße, auch von Jim!

Deine Sarah (your signed first name)

Prounciation

leebay maaria,

uebayr daainayn letsten breef haabayn vear oonz zayr gefreut. Toot mear laait, das ikh shon laange nikht geantvortet haabay, aabayr noon endlish bikomst du mal veedayr aain lebenstsaaishen fon oonz.

Vee du shon vaaist, vaar Jim draai vokhayn laang in aaziayn aauf geshaeftsraaizay. Daa musstay ikh tsu haauzay fast alays maakhayn unt kaam nee datsu, dear tsu shraaibayn. Aabayr mitlervaailay laeuft fast alles baai oonz veedayr normaal unt ikh haabay aain bisshayn tsaait, oom tsooar feder tsu begraaifen.

Am mitvokh vaaren vear baai Baarbaraa unt Dan tsum aabentesen. Zee laasen aaukh gruesayn unt hofen dikh veedayr im zomayr in Berlin tsu bezookhayn. Dan aarbaaitet imayr nokh baai...

Shoenay gruesay, aaukh von Jim!

Daainay, Sarah

More Closing Phrases & Formulae:

Alles Liebe - All my/our love, with love

Herzliche Grüße - Best wishes/Yours/Regards

Liebe Grüße und Küsse - Love and kisses

Viele liebe Grüße - Yours

Personal Letter/English Translation

Cactus City, the 25th of Nov. 2004

Dear Maria,

We were so glad to get your last letter! I'm sorry it has taken so long for me to reply, but now once again you're finally getting some indication that we're still alive.

As you already know, Jim was traveling in Asia on business for three weeks, so I had to do almost everything here at home, and never could find the time to write you. But in the meantime, almost everything here is running "normally" again, and I have a little time to set pen to paper.

On Wednesday we had dinner at Barbara and Dan's. They say hello and are hoping to visit you again in Berlin this summer. Dan is still working at...

Best wishes - from Jim, too!

Your Sarah

Personal Letter Phrases: These phrases are only appropriate for personal correspondence, not in formal or business situations!

General Phrases:

Thank you for your letter.
Vielen Dank für deinen Brief.
feelayn daank fuer daainayn breef

It was good to hear from you again.
Ich habe mich gefreut, wieder von dir zu hören.
ikh haabay mish gayfreut, veedayr fon dear tsu hoerayn

I'm sorry that I haven't written for so long.
Tut mir Leid, dass ich so lange nicht geschrieben habe.
tut mear laait, das ikh zo laangay nikht gayshreebayn haabay

Please don't be mad at me for...
Sei mir bitte nicht böse, dass ich...
zaai mear bitay nisht boezay, das ikh...

Closing Remarks:

Give my regards/love to Maria and Hans
Liebe Grüße an Maria und Hans
leebay gruesay an Maaria unt Haans

Tell them how much I miss them.
Sag ihnen, wie sehr sie mir fehlen.
zaag ihnayn, vee zayr zee mear faylayn

Tell her/him how much I miss her/him.
Sag ihr/ihm, wie sehr sie/er mir fehlt
zaag ihr/ihm, vee zayr zee/er mear faylt

Please write again soon!
Schreib mal wieder!
shraaib mal veedayr

Let us hear from you now and then.
Lasst ab und zu wieder von dir hören.
laast ab unt tsu fon dear hoerayn

Chapter 5

Professional letter writing

Tourist Office Enquiry:-

Johann Mustermann
Goethestraße 15
54321 Entenheim

25. Mai 2004

Verkehrsverein Kirchdorf e.V.
Hauptstr. 45
23451 Kirchdorf

Betreff: Hotels und Pensionen in Kirchdorf

Sehr geehrte Damen und Herren,
würden Sie mir freundlicherweise eine Liste der Hotels und Pensionen (der mittleren Kategorie) am Ort zusenden?

Daneben bin ich an Informationen über Busfahrten zu den Sehenswürdigkeiten der Umgebung im Juli interessiert.
Vielen Dank im Voraus!

Mit freundlichen Grüßen
[signature]
Johann Mustermann

Professional Writing

Pronunciation

Yohan Moostayrmaan
Goetheshtrasay 15
54321 Entenhaaim,

Fuenfuntsvaantsigten maai, 2004

ferkehrsferaain kirshdorf e.v.
haauptshtrasay 45
23451 kirshdorf

betref: hotels unt penseeonayn in kirshdorf

zayr geayhrte daamen unt heren,

vuerdayn zee mear froendlishayrvaaizay aainay listay dayr hotels unt penseeonayn (dayr mitlerayn kaategorie) am ort tsuzenden?

Daaneben bin ikh an Informatsionen uebayr boosfaahrtayn tsu dayn zehensvuerdishkaaitayn dayr oomgebung in yuli intayrayseart. feelayn daank im foraaus!

Mit froendlishen gruesayn,

[signaatooar]

Yohaan Moostayrmaan

Professional Letter/English Translation

Tourist Office Enquiry

Johann Mustermann
Goethe strape 15
54321 Entenheim

25 Mai, 2004

Verkehr verein kirchdorf e.v.
Hauptstr 45
23451 kirchdorf

Sub: Hotels and boarding houses in kirshdorf

Dear Sir/Madam,

Would you please send me the list of middle category hotels and boarding houses of the place?

Besides, I would like to be informed on the bus service to the tourist places of the surrounding.

Thank you very much in anticipation

[Signature]

Johann Mustermann

Part-IV
Chapter 1

Elementary Conversation

Do you speak German/English?
Sprechen Sie Deutsch/Englisch?
shprekhen zee doiach/aynglish

(Repeat) Once again, please.
Noch einmal, bitte.
nokh aainmal bitay

What did you say?
Wie bitte?
vee bitay

More slowly, please.
Langsamer, bitte.
laangzaamer bitay

Please repeat that.
Bitte Wiederholen Sie!
bitay veedayrholen zee

I don't understand.
Ich verstehe nicht.
ikh fershtehay nisht

I have a question.
Ich habe eine Frage.
ikh haabay aainay fraagay

How do you say...?
Wie sagt man...?
vee zaagt man

I don't know.
Ich weiß nicht.
ikh vaais nisht

On the contrary! / Yes. (in reply to a negative question)
Doch!
dokh

Where is/are...?
Wo ist/sind...?
vo ist/zint

When? - who? - how? - why? - what?
wann? - wer? - wie?- warum? - was
van - vayr - vee - vaarum - vaas

Okay!
Schon gut!
shon gut

I have no... / I don't have any...
Ich habe kein(e)...
ikh haabay kaainay

I don't have any money.
Ich habe kein Geld.
ikh haabay kaainay gelt

Chapter 2

At the Railway Station

Hello, I'd like a ticket to Leipzig, please.
Guten Tag. Ich hätte gern eine Fahrkarte nach Leipzig.
gutayn taak, ikh haettay gayrn aainay faarkaartay naakh laaiptsig

Single or return?
Einfach oder hin und zurück?
aainfaakh odayr hin unt tsuruek

A return ticket, please.
Eine Rückfahrkarte, bitte.
aainay rueckfaarkaartay bitay

When do you want to go?
Wann möchten Sie fahren?
van moeshtayn zee faarayn

Today on the next train, coming back in five days.
Heute mit dem nächsten Zug hin und in fünf Tagen wieder zurück.
heutay mit daym naekhstayn tsug hin unt in fuenf taagayn veedayr tsuruek

When does the next train leave?
Wann fährt der nächste Zug ab?
van faert dayr naekhstay tsug ab

At 12:51 from platform 1. The train arrives in Leipzig at four o'clock.
Um zwölf Uhr einunfünfzig vom Gleis eins. Der Zug kommt um sechzehn Uhr in Leipzig an.
oom tswoelf oohr aainuntfuenftsig fom glaais aains. Der tsug komt oom zaykhtsayn oohr in laaiptsig an

Do I have to change trains?
Muss ich umsteigen?
mus ikh oomshtaaigayn

Yes, change at Jüterbog.
Ja, steigen Sie in Jüterbog um.
yaa shtaaigayn zee in yuetayrbog oom

Would you like to reserve a seat?
Möchten Sie einen Platz reservieren?
moeshtayn zee aainayn plaats rayzayrvierayn

Yes, please. Non-smoker, and a window seat.
Ja, bitte. Nichtraucher, Fensterplatz.
yaa bitay, nishtraaukhayr, faynstayrplaats

Ok. That's 26 Euros. In Ordnung.
Das macht sechsundzwanzig Euro. in ordnung.
das maakht zekhsuntsvaantsig oyero

There you are.
Bitte sehr.
bitay zayr

Chapter 3

Taking a Taxi

Taxi! Good evening. Are you free?
Taxi! Guten Abend. Sind Sie frei?
taaxi, gutayn taak, zint zee fraai

Yes.
Ja.
yaa

Where to?
Wohin, bitte?
vohin bitay

To the New National Gallery.
Zur Neuen Nationalgalerie.
tsooar noyan naatsionaalgaalayree

Is that at Potsdamer Platz?
Ist das am Potsdamer Platz?
ist das am potsdaamayr plaats

Exactly.
Genau.
gaynaau

Ok, we're here.
So, wir sind da.
zo vear zint daa

Great. Many thanks.
Prima. Vielen Dank.
primaa, feelayn daank

Eight Euros, please.
Acht Euro, bitte.
aakht oyero bitay

Ten Euros. Keep the change.
Zehn Euro. Stimmt so.
tsayn oyero. Shtimt zo

Thank you. Have fun.
Danke. Viel Spaß.
daankay, feel shpas

Good bye.
Auf Wiedersehen.
aauf veedayrzayn

Chapter 4

At a Hotel

Good morning.
Guten Morgen.
gutayn morgayn

Good morning.
Guten Morgen.
gutayn morgayn

Do you have a room available at the beginning of August?
Haben Sie Anfang August ein Zimmer frei?
haabayn zee anfaang augoost aain tsimayr fraai

A single room or double room?
Einzelzimmer oder Doppelzimmer?
aaintsayl tsimayr oder dopayltsimayr

A single room, please.
Einzelzimmer, bitte.
aayntsayl tsimayr bitay

For how many nights?
Wie viele Nächte?
vee feelay naeshtay

Four nights. From the fourth to the eighth of August.
Vier Nächte. Vom vierten bis zum achten Augoost.
fear naekhtay. Fom feartayn bis tsum aakhtayn augoost

Just a moment, please.
Moment, bitte.
moment bitay

Yes, we have a room available. Your name please.
Ja, wir haben ein Zimmer frei.
Ihr Name bitte.

Yaa, vear haabayn aain tsimayr fraai.
ihr naame bitay

Chapter 5

At the Bank

Where is the nearest bank?
Wo ist die nächste Bank?
vo ist dee naekhstay baank

When does the bank open?
Wann öffnet die Bank?
van oefnayt dee baank

I would like to draw money.
Ich möchte Geld abheben.
ikh moeshtay gelt abhaybayn

Kindly change this money into Euro.
Bitte, wechseln Sie das Geld in Euro.
bitay, waykhseln zee das geld in oyero

Kindly examine this signture.
Bitte, prüfen Sie dies Untershrift.
bitay pruefayn zee diez oontayrshrift

Chapter 6

A Telephone Conversation

Sanjay (S) calls up his friend Hans (H).
Sanjay (S) ruft sein Freund Hans (H) an.
sanjay rooft zaain freond haans an.

S: Sanjay here. Can I speak to Hans please?
Hier Sanjay. Kann ich bitte Hans sprechen?
Hier sanjay. Kaan ikh bitay haans shprekhen

H: I am myself there on the phone. Good day, Sanjay. It is realy nice to receive your call once again.
Ich bin selbst am Apparat. Guten Tag, Sanjay. Schön, dass du endlich einmal wieder anrufst.
Ikh bin zelbst am apparaat. Gutayn taak, Sanjay. Shoen das du endlish aainmal veedayr anroofst

S: You know that I had gone home, because my mother was sick. I returned yesterday only.
Du weisst, dass ich nach Haus gefahren bin, weil meine Mutter krank war. Ich bin gestern zurückgekommen.
du waais, das ikh naakh Haauzay gefaahrayn bin, waail maainay mutar kraank war. Ikh bin gaystayrn tsurueckgaykomayn

H: And how is your mother now?
Und wie geht es deine Mutter jetzt?
unt vee gayt es daainay mutar yetst

S: Thank you, much better.
Danke, viel besser.
daankay feel baysayr

H: And what are you doing now? Can't you drop in? What about the evening?
Und was machst du jetzt? Kannst du nicht mal vorbeikommen? Wie ist es mit heute abend?
unt vaas maakhst du yetzt? Kaanst du nisht mal forbaaikomayn? Vee ist es mit heutay aabaynt

S: That's why I called you up. I'm free and would like to come.
Deshalb habe ich angerufen. Ich habe nichts vor and komme gern.
dayshaalb haabay ikh angerufayn. Ikh haabay nishts foar unt komay gayrn

H: It's my pleasure.
Also dann bis gleich! Ich freue mich schon.
alzo dan bis glaaish. Ikh freue mish shon

Chapter 7

Conversation with a Native Speaker

Hello, may I introduce myself? I'm Andrew Taylor.
Hallo, darf ich mich vorstellen? Ich bin Andrew Taylor.
hallo, daarf ikh mich forstaylayn? Ikh bin andrew taaylor

Pleased to meet you.
Angenehm.
angaynayhm

Are you from India or Pakistan?
Kommen Sie aus Indien oder aus Pakistan?
komayn zee aaus Indien oder aaus Pakistan

No, I'm from Nepal.
Nein, ich komme aus Nepal.
naain ikh kommay aaus nepal.

And you, are you from Germany?
Und Sie, kommen Sie aus Deutschland?
unt zee, komen zee aaus deutschlaand

Yes, I'm from Berlin.
Ja, ich komme aus Berlin.
yaa, ikh komay aaus berlin

Do you live in Berlin as well?
Wohnen Sie auch in Berlin?
vonen zee aaukh in berlin

Yes, I live in Prenzlauer Berg.
Ja, ich wohne in Prenzlauer Berg.
yaa, ikh vohnay in prentslaauer bayrg

And where do you live?
Und wo wohnen Sie?
unt vo vohnen zee

I live in Mitte. You speak German very well.
Ich wohne in Mitte. Sie sprechen sehr gut Deutsch.
ikh vohnay in mittay, zee shprekhayn zayr gut doiach

Thank you.
Danke.
daankay

Chapter 8

Discussing Weather

It's very warm today, isn't it?
Es ist sehr warm heute, nicht wahr?
es ist zayr vaarm heutay, nisht vaar

Yes, it's at least thirty-two degrees!
Ja, wir haben bestimmt zweiunddreißig Grad!
yaa, vear haabayn beshtimmt tsvaaiuntdraaissig graad

I'm from Munich. Is it always this hot here in the summer?
Ich komme aus München. Ist es immer so heiß hier im Sommer?
ikh komay aaus muenshen. Ist es imayr zo haais heear im zomayr

Not always. It's often rather cloudy.
Nicht immer. Manchmal ist es auch bewölkt.
nisht imayr. Manshmal ist es aaukh bewoelkt

In Munich it's often warm and dry in the summer.
In München ist es im Sommer oft heiß und trocken.
in muenshen ist es im zomayr oft haais unt trokayn

Ah, headache-weather.
Ah, Kopfschmerz-Wetter.
aah, kopfshmayrts-vetayr

Exactly!
Genau!
gayŋaau

Tomorrow we're going walking. Do you know what th weather'll be like tomorrow?
Morgen machen wir eine Wanderung. Wissen Sie, wie das Wetter morgen ist?
morgayn maakhayn vear aainay waandayrung. Wissayn zee, vee dass waytayr morgayn ist

I think a bit cool and windy.
Ich glaube, ziemlich kühl und windig.
ikh glaaubay, tsiemlich kuehl unt windig

It will remain rather changeable all week.
Diese Woche bleibt es recht wechselhaft.
diezay vokhay blaaibt es resht wekhselhaaft

As long as it doesn't rain ...
Solange es nicht regnet...
zolaangay es nisht raygnayt...

Chapter 9

Driving in Germany

Oh, my tank's almost empty. I need a petrol station.
Oh, mein Tank ist fast leer. Ich brauche eine Tankstelle.
oh, maain taank ist fast leer, ikh braaukhay aainay taankshtaylay

I think there's one at the end of the street.
Ich glaube, da ist eine am Ende der Straße.
ikh glaaubay, daa ist aainay am enday der shtrasay

Look, there's a petrol station on the left.
Schau mal, da links ist die Tankstelle.
shaaumal, daa links ist dee taankshtayllay

Oh, good.
Oh, gut.
oh, gut

Pump number five, please. Ah, I need some engine oil.
Säule Nummer fünf, bitte. Ah, ich brauche auch noch Motorenöl.
zaeulay noomayr fuenf bitay. Aah, ikh braaukhay aaukh nokh motorenoel

There, behind you on the shelf.
Da, hinter Ihnen, auf dem Regal.
daa, hintayr ihnen, aauf daym raygal

That's 30 Euros, please.
Das macht dreißig Euro, bitte.
das maakht draaissig oyero, bitay

I also need some air for the tyres. Do you have a pump?
Ich brauche noch Luft für die Reifen. Haben Sie eine Luftsäule?
ikh braaukhay nokh looft fuer dee raaifayn. Haabayn zee aainay looftzaeulay

Yes, it's just left of the entrance.
Ja, sie ist gleich links von der Einfahrt.
yaa, zee ist glaaish links fon dayr aainfaahrt

Thank you.
Danke.
daankay

Chapter 10

At a Marketplace

Can I help you?
Kann ich helfen?
kan ikh haylfayn

Yes. I like that car there. How much does it cost?
Ja. Das Auto da gefällt mir. Wie viel kostet es?
yaa, das aauto daa gayfaelt mear, vee feel kostayt es

The green car? Eight euros.
Das grüne Auto? Acht Euro.
das gruenay aauto? Aakht oyero

And this one?
Und das da?
unt das daa

This costs 60 euros.
Das kostet sechzig Euro.
das kostet zaykhtsig oyero

Oh, that's a bit expensive.
Oh, das ist ziemlich teuer.
oh, das ist tsimlish teuayr

How much do you want to spend?
Wie viel möchten Sie ausgeben?
vee feel moeshtayn zee aausgaybayn

Around 5 euros.
So fünf Euro.
zo fuenf oyero

We have the Berlin bear in different sizes and colours.
Wir haben den Berliner Bären in verschiedenen Größen und Farben.
vear haabayn dayn bayrlinayr baerayn in fersheedaynayn groesayn unt faarbayn

The big one costs 16 Euros and the small one six Euros.
Der große kostet sechzehn Euro und der kleine sechs Euro.
dayr grosay kostayt zaykhtsen oyero unt dayr klaainay zaykhs oyero

Ok, I'll take the small white one.
Ok, ich nehme den kleinen weißen.
ok, ikh nehme dayn klaainen waaisayn

That's six Euros.
Das macht sechs Euro.
das maakht zaykhs oyero

Thank you. Can you wrap it for me?
Danke. Können Sie es für mich einpacken?
daankay. Koenayn zee es fuer mish aainpaakayn

Yes, no problem.
Ja, kein Problem.
yaa, kaain problaym

Chapter 11

In a Restaurant

The menu, please
Die Speisekarte, bitte.
dee spaayzaykaartay bitay

Here you are.
Bitte schön.
bitay shoen

Thank you very much.
Danke sehr.
daankay zayr

Today we have duck.
Heute haben wir Ente.
heutay haabayn vear entay

I'm sorry, but I don't eat fish or meat.
Es tut mir leid, aber ich esse keinen Fisch und kein Fleisch.
es toot mear laait, aabayr ikh esse kaainayn fish unt kaain flaaish

We also have vegetarian dishes.
Wir haben auch vegetarische Gerichte.
vear haabayn aaukh vaygaytaarishay gayrishtay

Ah, that's good.
Ah, das ist gut.
aah, das ist gut

What are you having?
Was nimmst du?
vaas nimst du

I don't like duck. I think I'll have the vegetable plate. And you?
Ente mag ich nicht. Ich glaube, ich nehme die Gemüseplatte. Und du?
entay maag ikh nisht. Ikh glaaubay, ikh nehmay dee gaymuezayplaatay. Unt du

Mmm, I don't know. Is the tagliatelle made with meat?
Mmh, ich weiß nicht. Ist die Tagliatelle mit Fleisch?
mmh ikh vaais nisht. Ist dee taagliataylay mit flaaish

No, it's without meat, only with vegetables.
Nein, die ist ohne Fleisch, nur mit Gemüse.
naain dee ist ohnay flaaish, nooar mit gaymuezay

Ok, I'll take the tagliatelle.
Ok, ich nehme die Tagliatelle.
ok, ikh nehmay dee taagliaatayllay

Would you also like bread with it?
Möchten Sie auch Brot dazu?
moeshtayn zee aaukh brot daatsu

Yes, please.
Ja, bitte.
yaa bitay

Thank you.
Danke.
daankay

Chapter 12

At a Cafe

Excuse me? What are you having?
Entschuldigung? Was essen Sie da?
entshuldigung, vaas esayn zee daa?

I'm having a piece of chocolate cake.
Ich esse ein Stück Schokoladentorte.
ikh esay aain stueck shokolaadayntortay

And you?
Und Sie?
unt zee

Apple cake.
Apfelkuchen.
aapfaylkookhayn

And what are you drinking?
Und was trinken Sie?
unt vaas trinkayn zee

Normally I drink coffee, but today I'm having tea.
Normalerweise trinke ich Kaffee, aber heute trinke ich Tee.
normaalayrvaayzay trinkay ikh kaafay, aabayr heutay trinkay ikh tay

And you? Are you having a piece of cake too?
Und Sie? Essen Sie auch ein Stück Kuchen?
unt zee? Esayn zee aaukh aain stueck kookhayn

I'm having a piece of strawberry cake with cream and I'm drinking a cup of coffee.
Ich esse ein Stück Erdbeerkuchen mit Sahne und trinke eine Tasse Kaffee.
ikh esay aain stueck erdbayrkookhayn mit zaanay unt trinkay aainay taasay kaafay

Yes, please?
Bitte schön?
bitay shoen

A piece of apple cake and a cup of coffee, please.
Ein Stück Apfelkuchen und eine Tasse Kaffee, bitte.
aayn stueck aapfelkookhayn unt aainay taassay kaafay, bitay

There you are. Your apple cake and your coffee. Enjoy your meal.
Bitte schön. Ihr Apfelkuchen und Ihr Kaffee. Guten Appetit.
bitay shoen. Ihr aapfaylkukhayn unt ihr kaafay. Gutayn aapaytit

Thank you very much.
Danke schön.
daankay shoen

Chapter 13

Sports (Ski)

I'm a beginner (male/female).
Ich bin Anfänger/Anfängerin.
ikh bin anfaengayr/anfaengayrin

I'm advanced (male/female).
Ich bin Fortgeschrittener/Fortgeschrittene.
ikh bin fortgeshrittaynayr/fortgeshritaynayrin

I'd like to try snowboarding/cross-country ski-ing.
Ich möchte gern mal snowboarden/Langlaufski fahren.
ikh moeshtay gayrn mal snowboarden/laanglaaufskifaahrayn

I'd like a (family) lift pass for a week, please.
Ich möchte gern einen Familienskipass/Skipass für eine Woche, bitte.
ikh moeshtay gayrn aainayn faamiliaynskipaas/skipaas fuer aainay vokhay, bitay

What's the snow like?
Wie ist der Schnee?
vee ist dayr shnee

It's good/icy/powdery/soft.
Er ist gut/verharscht/pulverig/luschig.
ayr ist gut/fayrhaarsht/pulfayrig/lushig

Where's the next refuge?
Wo ist die nächste Zuflucht?
vo ist dee naekhstay Tsuflukht

Is it open/closed?
Ist es offen/geschlossen?
ist es ofayn/gayshlosayn

I've lost my (ski) sticks/lift pass/board.
Ich habe meine Skistöcke/meinen Skipass/mein Board verloren.
ikh haabay maainay skistoekay/maainayn skipaas/maain board ferlorayn

Avalanche!
Lawinengefahr!
laavinayngefaahr

Help!
Hilfe!
hilfay

Are you ok?
Bist du ok?
bist du ok

I've hurt my arm/leg/neck/ankle/shoulder.
Ich habe meinen Arm/mein Bein/meinen Knöchel/meine Schulter verletzt.
ikh haabay maainayn aarm/maain Baain/maainayn knoekhayl/ maainay shultayr fayrletst

Sorry, I'm still learning!
Entschuldigung, ich lerne noch!
entshuldigung ikh lerne nokh

What a poser!
Was für ein Angeber!
vaas fuer aain angeber

Part-V
Chapter 1

Nouns and Gender

Rules:

1. German nouns (a person, place or thing, Substantive) are very easy to spot: they always begin with a CAPITAL letter! German is the only world language that capitalizes all nouns. German nouns must begin with a capital letter. Whether we are talking about a simple tree (ein Baum) or Deutsche Bank, any noun is capitalized in German.
2. The other important thing for English-speakers to understand about German nouns is the matter of gender. German nouns parallel he, she and it (er, sie, es) by also being masculine (der - dayr), feminine (die - dee) or neuter (das - dass). We can see the parallel very clearly by the ending letters for each article/ pronoun: der = er, die = sie, das = es.
3. Der, die and das are the same as "the" in English – the DEFINITE ARTICLE. In German the definite article is much more important than it is in English. For one thing, it is used more often. In English we might say: "Nature is wonderful." In German, the article would also be included: "Die Natur ist wunderschön." So knowing which article to use becomes even more important!
3. The INDEFINITE ARTICLE ("a" or "an" in English) is **ein** or **eine** in German. **Ein** basically means "one" and like the definite article, it indicates the gender of the noun it goes with (eine or ein). For a feminine noun, only **eine** can be used (in the

nominative case). For masculine or neuter nouns, only **ein** is correct.

4. Gender is sometimes natural – der Mann/ein Mann (man, *masc.*), die Frau/eine Frau (woman, *fem.*), but more often it is not: das Mädchen (girl, neuter).
5. All nouns, of any gender, become **die** in the plural. (Ein can't be plural, but other so-called ein-words can: keine [none], meine [my], seine [his], etc.).

Substantive Nouns		
NOMINATIVE SINGULAR		
Artikel	**Gender**	**Sample Nouns**
der ein	masc.	der Bahnhof (train station), Sohn (son), Vater (father), Wagen (car), Zug (draft, parade, train)
die eine	fem.	die Anlage (installation, park), Dame (lady), Festung (fortress), Gesundheit (health), Luft (air)
das ein	neut.	das Boot (boat), Dach (roof), Geld (money), Jahr (year), Kino (cinema, movie theater), Radio

NOMINATIVE PLURAL		
Artikel	**Gender**	**Sample Nouns (Plurals)**
die keine meine	**plur.**	die Bücher (books), Dächer (roofs), Fenster (windows), Jahre (years), Radios, Söhne (sons), Zeitungen (newspapers)

Chapter 2

German Subordinating Conjunctions

English	German	Pronunciation
as, when	als	als
before	bevor	before
until	bis	bis
as/since	da	daa
so that	damit	daamit
that	dass	das
before	ehe	ehay
in case	falls	faals
while	indem	indaym
after	nachdem	naakhdaym
whether, if	ob	ob
although	obgleich	obglaaish
although	obschon	obschon
although	obwohl	obvohl
since (time)	seit/seitdem	zaaitdaym
as soon as	sobald	zobaalt
so that	so dass	zo das
as long as	solang(e)	zolaangay
despite	trotzdem	trotsdaym
while	während	vaehraynd
because	weil	vaail
if, whenever	wenn	ven

Note: All of the interrogative words (wann, wer, wie, wo, usw.) can also be used as subordinating conjunctions.

Chapter 3

German Modal Verbs

Modal Verbs/Modalverben :

PRÄSENS (Present)	PRÄTERITUM (Past)	PERFEKT (Pres. Perfect)
DÜRFEN - be allowed/permitted, may		
ich darf I may (am permitted)	ich durfte I was allowed	ich habe gedurft I was allowed
du darfst you may	du durftest you were allowed	du hast gedurft you were allowed
er/sie darf he/she may	er/sie durfte he/she was allowed	er/sie hat gedurft he/she was allowed
wir/Sie/sie dürfen we/you/they may	wir/Sie/sie durften we/you/they were allowed	wir/Sie/sie haben gedurft we/you/they were allowed
ihr dürft you (pl.) may	ihr durftet you (pl.) were allowed	ihr habt gedurft you (pl.) were allowed

KÖNNEN - be able, can		
ich kann I can, am able	ich konnte I could	ich habe gekonnt I could
du kannst you can	du konntest you could	du hast gekonnt you could
er/sie kann he/she can	er/sie konnte he/she could	er/sie hat gekonnt he/she could
wir/Sie/sie können we/you/they can	wir/Sie/sie konnten we/you/they could	wir/Sie/sie haben gekonnt we/you/they could
ihr könnt you (pl.) can	ihr konntet you (pl.) could	ihr habt gekonnt you (pl.) could
MÖGEN - like, want, may		
ich mag I like	ich mochte I liked	ich habe gemocht I liked
du magst you like	du mochtest you liked	du hast gemocht you liked
er/sie mag he/she likes	er/sie mochte he/she liked	er/sie hat gemocht he/she liked
wir/Sie/sie mögen we/you/they like	wir/Sie/sie mochten we/you/they liked	wir/Sie/sie haben gemocht we/you/they liked
ihr mögt you (pl.) like	ihr mochtet you (pl.) could	ihr habt gemocht you (pl.) could

Modal Verbs in Various Tenses With sample sentences:

1. dürfen (to be permitted, may)

Present:

May I smoke?
Darf ich rauchen?
daarf ikh raaukhayn

Past:

He wasn't permitted to do that.
Er durfte das nicht.
ayr doorftay das nisht

Pres. Perfect/Perfekt:

He was not permitted to park there.
Er hat dort nicht parken dürfen.
ayr hat dort nisht paarkayn duerfayn

Past Perfect/Plusquamperfekt:

We had been allowed to do that back then.
Wir hatten das damals machen dürfen.
vear hatayn das damals maakhayn duerfayn

Future/Futur:

We will be allowed to do that.
Wir werden das machen dürfen.
vear vayrdayn das maakhayn duerfayn

Sample Idiomatic Expressions:

May I help you?
Was darf es sein? (store clerk)
vaas daarf es zaain

If you please.
Wenn ich bitten darf.
ven ikh bitayn daarf

2. können (to be able, can, know):

Present:

He can drive well.
Er kann gut fahren.
ayr kan gut faarayn

Past:

He couldn't stand her.
Er konnte sie nicht leiden.
ayr kontay zee nisht laaidayn

Pres. Perfect/Perfekt:

He couldn't stand her.
Er hat sie nicht leiden können.
ayr hat zish nisht laaidayn koenayn

Past Perfect/Plusquamperfekt:

He had not been able to stand her.
Er hatte sie nicht leiden können.
ayr hatay zee nisht laaidayn koenayn

Future/Futur:

He won't be able to stand her.
Er wird sie nicht leiden können.
ayr vird zee nisht laaidayn koenayn

Sample Idiomatic Expressions:
You could be mistaken.
Sie könnten sich irren.
zee koentayn zish irayn

You can say that again.
Das kann man wohl sagen.
das kan man vohl zaagayn

He knows German. („can German")
Er kann Deutsch.
ayr kan doiach

1. müssen (to have to, must):
Present:
I have to speak German there.
Ich muss dort Deutsch sprechen.
ikh muss dort doiach spraykhayn

Past:
He didn't have to do it.
Er musste es nicht tun.
ayr musstay es nisht toon

Pres. Perfect/Perfekt:
We had to go by train.
Wir haben mit der Bahn fahren müssen.
vear haabayn mit dayr baan faahrayn muessayn

Future/Futur:
She will have to depart tomorrow.
Sie wird morgen abfahren müssen.
zee vird morgayn abfaahrayn muessayn

Sample Idiomatic Expressions:
I have to go home.
Ich muss nach Hause.
ikh muss naakh hausay

Is that really necessary?
Muss das sein?
muss das zaain

That's how it
So müsste es immer sein.
zo muesstay es immayr zaain

2. mögen (to like):
Present:
He likes the soup.
Er mag die Suppe.
ayr maag dee zoopay

Past:
He didn't like the city.
Er mochte die Stadt nicht.
ayr mokhtay dee shtat nikht

Pres. Perfect/Perfekt:
He didn't like the food.
Er hat das Essen nicht gemocht.
ayr hat das esayn nisht gaymokht

Future/Futur:
He'll like that.
Er wird das schon mögen.
ayr vird das schon moegayn

Sample Idiomatic Expressions:
That may be so.
Das mag wohl sein.
das maag vohl zaain

5. sollen (to be supposed to, should/ought to):
Present:
It's said that he's rich.
Er soll reich sein.
ayr zol raaish zaain

Past:
He was supposed to arrive yesterday.
Er sollte gestern ankommen.
ayr zoltay gaystayrn ankomayn

Pres. Perfect/Perfekt:
You should have called him.
Du hast ihn anrufen sollen.
du haast ihn nisht anrufayn zolayn

Future (in sense of):
He'll have that tomorrow.
Er soll das morgen haben.
ayr zoll das morgayn haabayn

Sample Idiomatic Expressions:
The book is said to be very good.
Das Buch soll sehr gut sein.
das bookh zoll zayr gut zaain

What's that supposed to mean?
Was soll das heißen?
vaas zoll das haaisayn

It won't happen again.
Es soll nicht wieder vorkommen.
es zoll nisht veedayr forkomayn

6. wollen (to want to, said to be) :

Present:

She doesn't want to go.
Sie will nicht gehen.
zee will nisht gayhayn

Past:

I wanted to read the book.
Ich wollte das Buch lesen.
ikh volltay das bookh layzayn

Pres. Perfect/Perfekt:

They have always wanted to see the movie.
Sie haben den Film immer sehen wollen.
zee haabayn dayn film imayr zayhayn vollayn

Past Perfect/Plusquamperfekt:

We had always wanted to see the movie.
Wir hatten den Film immer sehen wollen.
vear haatayn dayn film immayr zayhayn wollayn

Future/Futur:

He will want to go.
Er wird gehen wollen.
ayr vird gayhayn wollayn

Sample Idiomatic Expressions:

That's of little consequence.
Das will nicht viel sagen.
das will nisht feel zaagayn

That's not what he intended.
Das hat er nicht gewollt.
das hat ayr nisht gaywollt

Chapter 4

Aktiv/Passiv

ACTIVE/AKTIV:

I'm writing the letter.
Ich schreibe den Brief.
ikh shraaibay dayn breef

PASSIVE/PASSIV:

The letter is being written by me.
Der Brief wird von mir geschrieben.
dayr breef vird fon mear gayshreebayn

Rules:

1. To form the passive, German uses werden (to become) + the past participle, while English uses "to be."
2. The word "letter" (Brief) in the ACTIVE sentence is an object being acted upon (active) by the subject "I" (ich). In the PASSIVE sentence the former object (Brief) becomes the subject, while the former subject (I, ich) is now the agent (by me/von mir).
3. Only transitive verbs (those that take a direct object) can be made passive. The direct object (accusative case) in the active voice becomes the subject (nominative case) in the passive voice.

   Note: A passive voice sentence may or may not include the "agent" (by whom something was done). If the agent (by me, by Anna) is a person, it is expressed in German with a von-phrase: **von Anna** (by Anna). If the agent is not a person, then a durch-phrase is used: **durch den Wind** (by the wind). Here are some more color-coded examples, with and without the agent expressed:

ACTIVE/AKTIV:

The wind storm destroyed the building.
Der Sturm hat das Haus zerstört.
dayr sturm hat das house tsayrstoert

PASSIVE/PASSIV (no agent expressed)

The building was destroyed.
Das Haus ist zerstört worden.
das house ist tsayrstoert wordayn

PASSIVE/PASSIV (agent expressed)

The building was destroyed by the wind storm.
Das Haus ist durch den Sturm zerstört worden.
das house ist dursh dayn sturm tsayrstoert vordayn

"FALSE" PASSIVE (predicate adjective)

The building is destroyed.
Das Haus ist zerstört.
das house ist tsayrstoert

The building was destroyed.
Das Haus war zerstört.
das house vaar tsayrstoert

Rules: The ACTIVE verb form "hat zerstört" changes to "ist zerstört worden" in the PASSIVE.

Although the normal past participle of „werden“ is „(ist) geworden,“ when the past participle is used with another verb, it becomes „ist (zerstört) worden.“

If the ACTIVE sentence contains a past participle (i.e., “zerstört”), it will also appear, unchanged, in the PASSIVE sentence with “worden.”

The “false passive” example is NOT in the passive voice. The past participle “zerstört” is only being used as a predicate adjective, describing the condition of the building (“destroyed”).

A Newspaper Excerpt / Aus der Zeitung: Some slightly edited passive examples from a German newspaper:

A new shopping center should be opening this summer.
Ein neues Einkaufszentrum soll in diesem Sommer eröffnet werden.
aain noyays aainkaauftsayntrum zoll in diezaym zomayr eroefnayt vayrdayn.

He was chosen ,Mr. Germany 2001.
‘Er ist zum, Mr. Germany 2001‘ gewählt worden.
ayr ist tsum, Mr. Germany 2001 ‘gayvaehlt vordayn

For the time being no exact figures were given.
Es wurden zunächst keine genauen Zahlen genannt.
es vurdayn tsunaekhst kaainay gaynaauayn tsaalayn gaynaant.

On Tuesday in Berlin’s Bellevue Palace it was celebrated: Federal President Johannes Rau turned 70.

Am Dienstag wurde im Berliner Schloss Bellevue gefeiert: Bundespräsident Johannes Rau wurde 70 Jahre alt.

am deenstaag vurday im Bayrlinayr shloss bellevue gayfaairt: bundayspraezidaynt Yohaanays Raau vurday zeebtsig yaaray aalt.

Chapter 5

Prepositions and Cases

The following chart shows the four cases with the definite article (der, die, das), the indefinite article and the third-person pronouns (er, sie, es).

Definite Article (der, die, das)				
Case Fall	Masculine Männlich	Feminine Weiblich	Neuter Sächlich	Plural Mehrzahl
Nom	der	die	das	die
Akk	den	die	das	die
Dat	dem	der	dem	den
Gen	des	der	des	der
Indefinite Article (ein, mein, ihr)				
Case Fall	Masculine Männlich	Feminine Weiblich	Neuter Sächlich	Plural Mehrzahl
Nom	ein	eine	ein	Keine
Akk	einen	eine	ein	Keine
Dat	einem	einer	einem	Keinen
Gen	eines	einer	eines	keiner

Note: **keine** is the negative of **eine,** which has no plural form. But keine (no/none) can be used in the plural: "Er hat keine Bücher." (He has no books.) - "In Venedig gibt es keine Autos." (In Venice there are no cars.)

Prepositionen mit Accusativ:

There are two kinds of accusative prepositions: (1) those that are always accusative and never anything else, and (2) certain „two-way“ prepositions that can be either accusative or dative – depending on how they are used.

Here is a list of the accusative-only prepositions.

Accusative Prepositions		
English	**Deutsch**	**Pronunciation**
until, to	bis	bis
through, by	durch	doorsh
along, down	entlang	entlaang
for	für	fuer
against, for	gegen	gaygayn
without	ohne	ohnay
around, for; at (time)	um	oom

Examples:

Without money it won't work.
Ohne Geld geht's nicht.
ohnay gayld gayht es nisht

She is walking along the river.
Sie geht den Fluss **entlang**.
zee gayht dayn flus entlaang

He works for a big company.
Er arbeitet **für** ein große Firma.
ayr aarbaaitayt fuer aain grosay firmaa

We're driving through the city.
Wir fahren **durch** die Stadt.
vear faahrayn dursh dee shtat

Are you writing a letter to your father?
Schreibst du einen Brief **an** deinen Vater?
shraaibst du aainayn breef an daainayn faatar

Note:

1. The accusative preposition **entlang**, unlike the others, usually goes <u>after</u> its object, as in the example above.

2. The German preposition **bis** is technically an accusative preposition, but it's almost always used with a second preposition (bis zu, bis auf, etc.) in a different case, or without an article (bis April, bis Montag, bis Bonn).

Two-Way Prepositions Accusative/Dative		
Englisch	**Deutsch**	**Pronunciation**
at, on, to	an	an
at, to, on, upon	auf	aauf
behind	hinter	hintar
in, into	in	in
beside, near, next to	neben	nebayn

about, above, across, over	über	uebayr
under, among	unter	oontayr
in front of, before; ago (time)	vor	foar
between	zwischen	tsvishen

Rule: If there is motion towards something or a specific location, then usually that is **accusative**. If there is no motion at all or random motion going nowhere in particular, then that is usually **dative**.

Examples:

We're going to the movies/cinema. (motion towards)
Wir gehen ins Kino. (*in das, accus.*)
vear gayhayn ins kino

We're at the movies/cinema. (location)
Wir sind im Kino. (*in dem, dat.*)
vear zint im kino

Put/Lay the book on the table. (motion towards)
Legen Sie das Buch auf den Tisch. (*accusative*)
laygayn zee das bukh aauf daym tish

The book's lying on the table. (location)
Das Buch liegt auf dem Tisch. (*dative*)
das bukh leegt aauf daym tish

Prepositionen mit Dativ:

There are two kinds of dative prepositions: (1) those that are always dative and never anything else, and (2) certain „two-way" prepositions that can be **either dative or accusative** – depending on how they are used.

Examples:

We're going by train.
Mit der Bahn fahren wir.
mit dayr baan faahrayn vear

In my opinion it's too expensive.
Meiner Meinung **nach** ist es zu teuer.
maainayr maainung naakh ist es tsu teuayr

The hotel is across the train station.
Das Hotel ist dem Bahnhof **gegenüber**.
dass hotayl ist daym baanhof gaygaynuebayr

He works at a big company.
Er arbeitet **bei** einer großen Firma.
ayr aarbaaitayt baai aainayr grosayn firmaa

We're spending a week at the lake.
Wir verbringen eine Woche **am** See.
vear fayrbringayn aainay vokhay am zay

Note: In the second and third examples above that the object comes **before** the preposition. (With *gegenüber* this is optional.)

Dative Prepositions		
English	**Deutsch**	**Pronunciation**
from, out of	**aus**	aaus
except for, besides	**außer**	aausayr
at, near	**Bei**	baai
across from, opposite	**gegenüber**	gaygaynyebayr

with, by	mit	mit
after, to	nach	naakh
since (time), for	seit	zaait
by, from	von	fon
at, to	zu	tsu

Two-Way Prepositions
Dative/Accusative

English	Deutsch	Pronunciation
at, on, to	an	an
at, to, on, upon	auf	aauf
behind	hinter	hintar
in, into	in	in
beside, near, next to	neben	neben
about, above, across	über	uebayr
under, among	unter	oontyar
in front of, before; ago (time)	vor	foar
between	zwischen	tsvishayn

Rule: The basic rule for determining whether a two-way preposition should have an object in the accusative or dative case is **motion** (*wohin?*, where to?) versus **location** (*wo?*, where?, at rest). If there is motion towards something or a specific location, then usually that is **accusative**. If there is no motion at all or random motion going nowhere in particular, then that is usually **dative**.

Examples:

We're going to the movies/cinema. (motion towards)
Wir gehen ins Kino. (*in das, accus.*)
vear gayhayn ins kino.

We're at the movies/cinema. (location)
Wir sind im Kino. (*in dem, dat.*)
vear zint im kino.

Put/Lay the book on the table. (motion towards)
Legen Sie das Buch auf den Tisch. (*accusative*)
laygayn zee das bookh aauf dayn tish

The book's lying on the table. (location)
Das Buch liegt auf dem Tisch. (*dative*)
das bookh leegt aauf daym tish

Prepositionen mit Genitiv:

There are only a few common genitive prepositions in German, including: (**an**)**statt** (instead of), **trotz** (in spite of), **während** (during) and **wegen** (because of).

Examples:

During the week we work.
Während der Woche arbeiten wir.
vaehraynd dayr vokhay aarbaaitayn vear

In spite of the weather we're driving home today.
Trotz des Wetters fahren wir heute nach Hause.
trots days vetayrs faahrayn vear heutay naakh haauzay

Genitive Prepositions		
English	**Deutsch**	**Pronunciation**
instead of	(an)statt	an shtat
despite, in spite of	trotz	trots
during, in the course of	während	vaehrend
because of	wegen	vegayn

Verbs and Prepositions:

There are many German verbs and idiomatic verb phrases that use prepositions. For many **verb + preposition** expressions, one simply has to learn which case the verb uses, much as one has to learn the gender of a German noun.

With the exception of **an**, two-way prepositions with verbs usually take the accusative case. For instance, in verbal phrases, the two-way preposition **über** usually means "about" and is accusative. In contrast, most **an** verb phrases, such as **arbeiten an** (to work on), are dative. Unlike the other two-way prepositions, very few verb expressions with **an** are accusative. These include: **denken an** (think of), **glauben an** (believe in), **s. halten an** (hold to), and **s. erinnern an** (remember). In stock verb phrases, **über** is always accusative, **vor** is always dative (but not in other situations).

ABBREVIATIONS USED: A (accusative), **D** (dative), **etw** (etwas), **jdn** (*jemanden*, someone), **s.** (*sich*, reflexive verb), **s.o.** (someone), **s.t.** (something).

Verbs with Prepositions :

Prepositions Used with Verbs Präpositionen mit Verben		
Prep.	**Verb Phrase**	**Example**
an	**an** etw **arbeiten** D	He's working on a novel. **Er arbeitet an einem Roman.** ayr aarbaaitayt an aainaym romaan
an	**an** etw/jdn **denken** A	I think of him often. **Ich denke oft an ihn.** ikh daynkay oft an ihn
auf	**auf** etw **achten** A	You have to pay attention to the price. **Sie müssen auf den Preis achten.** zee muessayn aauf dayn praais aakhtayn
auf	**auf** etw **bestehen** D	He insisted on his rights. **Er hat auf seinen Rechten bestanden.** ayr hat aauf zaainayn raykhtayn bestaandayn
aus	**aus** etw **bestehen** D	His house is made of stone. **Sein Haus besteht aus Stein.** zzain house bestayht aaus staain

für	**für** etw **sorgen** A	The police strive for law and order. **Die Polizei sorgt für Recht und Ordnung.** dee politsaai zorgt fuer resht unt ordnung
in	**s. in** jdn **verlieben** A	He fell in love with her. **Er hat sich in sie verliebt.** ayr hat zish in zee fayrleebt
in	**s. in** etw/jdm **täuschen** D	He disappointed me. **Ich habe mich in ihm getäuscht.** ikh haabay mish in ihm gaytaeusht
mit	**mit** etw **rechnen** D	We didn't account for his stupidity. **Wir haben mit seiner Dummheit nicht gerechnet.** vear haabayn mit zaainayr dummhaait gayrayshnayt
nach	**nach** etw **riechen** D	It smells like/of gasoline. **Es riecht nach Benzin.** es reesht naakh bayntsin
über	**über** etw/jdn **urteilen** A	I can't judge his talent. **Ich kann nicht über sein Talent urteilen.** ikh kann nisht uebayr zaain taalaynt oortaailayn

über	**über** etw **verfügen** A	Do you have access to a computer? **Verfügst du über einen Rechner?** fayrfuegst du uebayr aainayn rayshnayr
um	**s. um** etw **bewerben** A	Are you applying for the position? **Bewirbst du dich um den Posten?** baywirbst du dish oom dayn postayn
von	**von** etw/jdm **distanzieren** D	They distanced themselves from him. **Sie haben sich von ihm distanziert.** zee haabayn zish fon ihm distaantsiert
vor*	jdn **vor** etw **retten** D	She saved him from the water. **Sie hat ihn vor dem Wasser gerettet.** zee hat ihn foar daym waasayr gayraytayt
zu	**zu** etw/jdm **stehen** D	Are you sticking by/with him? **Stehst du zu ihm?** stayhst du tsu ihm

Note: The German preposition in verbal idioms may or may not resemble the English preposition. In fact, in some German verbal phrases with a preposition there is no preposition at all in the English equivalent: **aufhören mit** (to stop doing something), **erinnern an** (to remember).

Chapter 6

Adjective

German adjectives, like English ones, usually go in front of the noun they modify: "der gute Mann" (the good man), "das große Haus" (the big house/building), "die schöne Dame" (the pretty lady). Unlike English adjectives, a German adjective in front of a noun has to have an ending (**-e** in the examples above). Just what that ending will be depends on several factors, including **gender** (der, die, das) and **case** (nominative, accusative, dative). But most of the time the ending is an **-e** or an **-en** (in the plural).

With **definite article** (der, die, das) - **Nominative case**			
Masculine **der**	Feminine **die**	Neuter **das**	Plural **die**
the new car der neu**e** Wagen dayr neuay vaagayn	the beautiful city die schön**e** Stadt dee shoenay stat	the old car das alt**e** Auto das altay aauto	the new books die neu**en** Bücher dee neuayn bueshayr
With **indefinite article** (eine, kein, mein) - **Nom. case**			
Masculine **ein**	Feminine **eine**	Neuter **ein**	Plural **keine**
a new car ein neu**er** Wagen aain neuayr vaagayn	a beautiful city eine schön**e** Stadt aainay shoenay stat	an old car ein alt**es** Auto aain altays aauto	no new books keine neuen Bücher kaainay neuayn buesher

Note: With **ein**-words, since the article may not tell us the gender of the following noun, the adjective ending often does this instead (**-es** = **das**, **-er** = **der**; see above).

As in English, a German adjective can also come **after** the verb (predicate adjective): "Das Haus ist groß." (The house is large.) In such cases the adjective will have NO ending.

Adjective Endings:
Accusative/Dative

The following chart shows the adjective endings for the **accusative** and **dative** cases with the definite articles (der, dem, der) and the indefinite articles (einen, einem, einer, keinen).

Accusative Case (Direct Object)			
Masculine **den**	Feminine **die**	Neuter **das**	Plural **die**
the new car den neu**en** Wagen dayn neuayn vaagayn	the beautiful city die schön**e** Stadt dee shoenay stat	the old car das alt**e** Auto das altay aauto	the new books die neu**en** Bücher dee neuayn buesher
Masculine **einen**	Feminine **eine**	Neuter **ein**	Plural **keine**
a new car einen neu**en** Wagen aainayn neuayn vaagayn	a beautiful city eine schön**e** Stadt aainay shoenay stat	an old car ein alt**es** Auto aain altays aauto	no new books keine neu**en** Bücher kaainay neuayn bueshayr

Dative Case (Indirect Object)			
Masculine **dem**	Feminine **der**	Neuter **dem**	Plural **den**
(to) the nice man dem nett**en** Mann daym netayn maan	(to) the beautiful woman der schön**en** Frau dayr shoenayn fraau	(to) the nice girl dem nett**en** Mädchen daym netayn maedshayn	(to) the man other people den anderen Leuten dayn andayrayn loitayn
Masculine **einem**	Feminine **einer**	Neuter **einem**	Plural **keinen**
(to) a nice man einem nett**en** Mann aainaym netayn maan	(to) a beautiful woman einer schön**en** Frau aainayr shoenayn fraau	(to) a nice girl einem nett**en** Mädchen aainaym netayn maedshayn	(to) no other people keinen andere**n** Leute**n** kaainayn andayrayn loitayn

Note: The adjective endings in the Genitive Case are the same as in the DATIVE - all **-en**!

Chapter 7

Subject-Verb Agreement

SEIN (to be)
Present Tense - *Präsens*

English	Deutsch	Pronunciation
SINGULAR		
I am	ich bin	ikh bin
you (fam.) are	du bist	du bist
he is	er ist	ayr ist
it is	es ist	es ist
she is	sie ist	zee ist
PLURAL		
we are	wir sind	vear zint
you (guys) are	ihr seid	ihr zaait
they are	sie sind	zee zint
you are	Sie sind	zee zint

Examples:

Are you Mr. Meier?
Sind Sie Herr Meier?
zint zee hayr maayayr

He's not here.
Er ist nicht da.
ayr ist nisht daa

SEIN

Compound Past Tense (Pres. Perfect) *Perfekt*

English	Deutsch	Pronunciation
SINGULAR		
I was	ich war	ikh vaar
you (fam.) were	du warst	du vaarst
he was	er war	ayr vaar
it was	es war	es vaar
she was	sie war	zee vaar
PLURAL		
we were	wir waren	vear vaaren
you (guys) were	ihr wart	ihr vaart
they were	sie waren	zee vaaren
you were	Sie waren	zee vaaren

English	Deutsch	Pronunciation
SINGULAR		
I was/have been	ich bin gewesen	ikh bin gevezayn
you (fam.) were/have been	du bist gewesen	du bist gevezayn
he was/has been	er ist gewesen	ayr ist gevezayn
she was/has been	sie ist gewesen	zee ist gevezayn
it was/has been	es ist gewesen	es ist gevezayn

PLURAL		
we were/have been	wir sind gewesen	vear zint gevezayn
you (guys) were/ have been	ihr seid gewesen	ihr zaait gevezayn
they were/have been	sie sind gewesen	zee zint gevezayn
you were/have been	Sie sind gewesen	zee zint gevezayn

SEIN

Past Perfect Tense *Plusquamperfekt*

English	**Deutsch**	**Pronunciation**
SINGULAR		
I had been	ich war gewesen	ikh vaar gevezayn
you (fam.) had been	du warst gewesen	du vaarst gevezayn
he had been	er war gewesen	ayr vaar gevezayn
it had been	es war gewesen	es vaar gevezayn
she had been	sie war gewesen	zee vaar gevezayn
PLURAL		
we had been	wir waren gewesen	vear vaaren gevezayn
you (guys) had been	ihr wart gewesen	ihr vaart gevezayn
they had been	sie waren gewesen	zee vaaren gevezayn
you had been	Sie waren gewesen	zee vaaren gevezayn

SEIN

FUTURE TENSE/ FUTUR

Note: The future tense, especially with **sein** is used much less in German than in English. Very often the present tense is used with an adverb instead. (Er kommt am Dienstag. = He'll arrive on Tuesday.)

SEIN

Future Tense - *Futur*

English	Deutsch	Pronunciation
SINGULAR		
I will be	ich werde sein	ikh verday zaain
you (fam.) will be	du wirst sein	du virst zaain
he will be	er wird sein	ayr vird zaain
it will be	es wird sein	es vird zaain
she will be	sie wird sein	zee vird zaain
PLURAL		
we will be	wir werden sein	vear verdayn zaain
you (guys) will be	ihr werdet sein	ihr verdayn zaain
they will be	sie werden sein	zee verdayn zaain
you will be	Sie werden sein	zee verdayn zaain

SEIN

Future Perfect - *Futur II*

English	Deutsch	Pronunciation
SINGULAR		
I will have been	ich werde gewesen sein	ikh verday gevezayn zaain
you (fam.) will have been	du wirst gewesen sein	du virst gevezayn zaain
he will have been	er wird gewesen sein	ayr vird gevezayn zaain
she will have been	sie wird gewesen sein	zee vird gevezayn zaain
it will have been	es wird gewesen sein	es vird gevezayn zaain
PLURAL		
we will have been	wir werden gewesen sein	vear verdayn gevezayn zaain
you (guys) will have been	ihr werdet gewesen sein	ihr verdayt gevezayn zaain
they will have been	sie werden gewesen sein	zee verdayn gevezayn zaain
you will have been	Sie werden gewesen sein	zee verdayn gevezayn zaain

HABEN

Present Tense - *Präsens*

English	Deutsch	Pronunciation
SINGULAR		
I have	ich habe	ikh haabay
you have	du hast	du hast
he has	er hat	ayr hat
she has	sie hat	zee hat
it has	es hat	es hat
PLURAL		
we have	wir haben	vear haabayn
you (guys) have	ihr habt	ihr haabt
they have	sie haben	zee haabayn
you have	Sie haben	zee haabayn

HABEN

Simple Past Tense – *Imperfekt*

English	Deutsch	Pronunciation
SINGULAR		
I had	ich hatte	ikh hatay
you had	du hattest	du hatayst
he had	er hatte	ayr hatay
she had	sie hatte	zee hatay
it had	es hatte	es hatay

PLURAL		
we had	wir hatten	vear hatayn
you (guys) had	ihr hattet	ihr hatayt
they had	sie hatten	zee hatayn
you had	Sie hatten	zee hatayn

HABEN
Compound Past Tense (Pres. Perfect) - *Perfekt*

English	Deutsch	Pronunciation
SINGULAR		
I had/have had	ich habe gehabt	ikh haabay gehaabt
you (fam.) had/ have had	du hast gehabt	du haast gehaabt
he had/has had	er hat gehabt	ayr hat gehaabt
she had/has had	sie hat gehabt	zee hat gehaabt
it had/has had	es hat gehabt	es hat gehaabt
PLURAL		
we had/have had	wir haben gehabt	vear haabayn gehaabt
you (guys) had/ have had	ihr habt gehabt	ihr haabt gehaabt
they had/have had	sie haben gehabt	zee haabayn gehaabt
you had/have had	Sie haben gehabt	zee haabayn gehaabt

HABEN

Past Perfect - *Plusquamperfekt*

English	Deutsch	Pronunciation
SINGULAR		
I had had	ich hatte gehabt	ikh hatay gehaabt
you (fam.) had had	du hattest gehabt	du hatayst gehaabt
he had had	er hatte gehabt	ayr hatay gehaabt
she had had	sie hatte gehabt	zee hatay gehaabt
it had had	es hatte gehabt	es hatay gehaabt
PLURAL		
we had had	wir hatten gehabt	vear hatayn gehaabt
you (guys) had had	ihr hattet gehabt	ihr hatayt gehaabt
they had had	sie hatten gehabt	zee hatayn gehaabt
you had had	Sie hatten gehabt	zee hatayn gehaabt

HABEN

Future Tense- *Futur*

English	Deutsch	Pronunciation
SINGULAR		
I will have	ich werde haben	ikh verday haabayn
you (fam.) will have	du wirst haben	du virst haabayn
he will have	er wird haben	ayr vird haabayn
she will have	sie wird haben	zee vird haabayn

PLURAL		
we will have	wir werden haben	vear verdayn haabayn
you (guys) will have	ihr werdet haben	ihr verdayt haabayn
they will have	sie werden haben	zee verdayn haabayn
you will have	Sie werden haben	zee verdayn haabayn

Chapter 8

CONJUGATIONS

Rules: 1. Each verb has a basic „infinitive“ („to“) form. The verb „to play“ in English is the infinitive form. („He plays“ is a conjugated form.) The German equivalent of „to play“ is **spielen**.

1. Each verb has a “stem” form, the basic part of the verb left after you remove the **-en** ending. For **spielen** the stem is **spiel- (spielen - en)**.
2. To conjugate the verb—that is, use it in a sentence—one must add the correct ending to the stem. Each „person“ (he, you, they, etc.) requires its own ending on the verb. In the present tense, German has a different ending for almost all of those verb situations.
3. German has no present progressive tense (“am going”/”are buying”). The German *Präsens* “ich kaufe” can be translated into English as “I buy” or “I am buying,” depending on the context.

Examples:

SPIELEN (to play)

English	Deutsch	Sample Sentence
SINGULAR		
I play	ich spiele	Ich spiele gern Basketball.
you(fam.)	du spielst	Spielst du Schach? (chess)play
he plays	er spielt	Er spielt mit mir. (with me)
she plays	sie spielt	Sie spielt Karten. (cards)
it plays	es spielt	Es spielt keine Rolle. (It doesn’t matter.)

PLURAL		
we play	wir spiel**en**	Wir spielen Basketball.
you (guys) play	ihr spiel**t**	Spielt ihr Monopoly?
they play	sie spiel**en**	Sie spielen Golf.
you play	Sie spiel**en**	Spielen Sie heute?

Note: Sie, formal „you," is both singular and plural.

ARBEITEN (to work)

English	**Deutsch**	**Sample Sentence**
SINGULAR		
I work	ich arbeit**e**	Ich arbeite am Samstag.
you (fam.) work	du arbeit**est**	Arbeitest du in der Stadt?
he works	er arbeit**et**	Er arbeitet mit mir. (with me)
she works	sie arbeit**et**	Sie arbeitet nicht.
it works	es arbeit**et**	—
PLURAL		
we work	wir arbeit**en**	Wir arbeiten zu viel.
you (guys) work	ihr arbeit**et**	Arbeitet ihr am Montag?
they work	sie arbeit**en**	Sie arbeiten bei BMW.
you work	Sie arbeit**en**	Arbeiten Sie heute?

Example of Stem-Changing Verbs

Note: In the examples below, **er** stands for all three third-person pronouns (er, sie, es). Stem-changing verbs only change in the **singular** (except for ich). Their plural forms are completely regular.

English	Deutsch	Sample Sentence
to travel	fahren	
he travels	er fährt	Er fährt nach Berlin. (He's traveling/going toBerlin.)
you travel	du fährst	Ich fahre nach Berlin. (I'm traveling/going to Berlin.)
to read	lesen	
he reads	er liest	Maria liest die Zeitung. (Maria's reading the newspaper.)
you read	du liest	Wir lesen die Zeitung. (We read the newspaper.)
to take	nehmen	
he takes	er nimmt	Karl nimmt sein Geld.
you take	du nimmst	(Karl's taking his money.)
		Ich nehme mein Geld. (I am taking my money)
to forget	vergessen	
he forgets	er vergisst	Er vergisst immer. (He always forgets.)
you forget	du vergisst	Vergiss es! / Vergessen Sie es! (Forget it!)

Twenty most important German Verbs

English	Deutsch	Sample Sentence
to be	sein	zaain
to have	haben	haabayn
to become	werden	verdayn
to be able/can	können	koenayn
to have to	müssen	muesayn
to want to	wollen	volayn
to like to	mögen	moegayn
to know	wissen	visayn
to make/do	machen	maakhayn
should	sollen	zolayn
to be called/ named	heißen	haaisayn
to say/tell	sagen	zaagayn
to go	gehen	gayhayn
to see	sehen	zayhayn
to give	geben	gaybayn
to come	kommen	komayn
to let/allow	lassen	laasayn
to find	finden	findayn
to stay/remain	bleiben	blaaibayn
to take	nehmen	nehmayn
to bring	bringen	bringayn

Chapter 9

The Article/Der Artikel

Rules:

1. Most world languages have nouns that are either masculine or feminine. German, besides capitalizing all nouns, goes them one better and adds a third gender: neuter. The masculine definite article ("the") is **der**, feminine is **die**, and neuter is **das**.

2. It's not the actual person, place or thing that has gender in German, but the WORD that stands for the actual thing. That's why a "car" can be either **das Auto** (neut.) or **der Wagen** (masc.).

3. Although nouns for people often follow natural gender, there are exceptions such as **das Mädchen**, girl. There are three different German words for "ocean" or "sea"—all a different gender: **der Ozean**, **das Meer**, **die See!**

4. And gender does not transfer well from one language to another. The word for "sun" is masculine in Spanish (*el sol*) but feminine in German (*die Sonne*). A German moon is masculine (*der Mond*), while a Spanish moon is feminine (*la luna*).

> **Note:** A good general rule for learning German vocabulary is to treat the article of a noun as an integral part of the word. Don't just learn *Garten* (garden), learn *der Garten*. Don't just learn *Tür* (door), learn *die Tür*. Not knowing a word's gender can lead to all sorts of other problems: *das Tor* is the gate or portal; *der Tor* is the fool.

German Noun Gender: Masculine - DER

Rule: When learning a German noun, one should always treat its article as an integral part of the word! Not *Wasser*, but *das Wasser*. Not *Hund*, but *der Hund*. However, it can be very helpful to know about the gender generalizations below.

Always Masculine (MÄNNLICH) (der/ein):

- Days, months, and seasons: *Montag, Juli, Sommer* (Monday, July, summer). The one exception is *das Frühjahr*, another word for *der Frühling*, spring.
- Points of the compass, map locations and winds: *Nordwest(en)* (northwest), *Süd(en)* (south), *der Föhn* (warm wind out of the Alps), *der Scirocco* (sirocco, a hot desert wind).
- Precipitation: *Regen, Schnee, Nebel* (rain, snow, fog/mist)
- Names of cars and trains: *der VW, der ICE, der Mercedes.* (But motorbikes and aircraft are feminine.)
- Words ending in *-ismus*: *Journalismus, Kommunismus, Synchronismus* (equal -ism words in English)
- Words ending in *-ner*: *Rentner, Schaffner, Zentner, Zöllner* (pensioner, [train] conductor, hundred-weight, customs collector). The feminine form adds *-in* (*die Rentnerin*).
- The basic „atmospheric“ elements that end in *-stoff*: *der Sauerstoff* (oxygen), *der Stickstoff* (nitrogen), *der Wasserstoff* (hydrogen), plus carbon *(der Kohlenstoff)*. The only other element (out of 112) that is masculine is *der Schwefel* (sulphur). All of the other chemical elements are neuter *(das Aluminium, Blei, Kupfer, Uran, Zink, usw.)*

Usually MASCULINE (der/ein):

- Agents (people who do something), most occupations and nationalities:

der Architekt, der Arzt, der Deutsche, der Fahrer, der Verkäufer, der Student, der Täter (architect, physician, German [person], driver, salesman, student, perpetrator).

The feminine form of these terms almost always ends in *-in* *die Architektin, die Ärztin, die Fahrerin, die Verkäuferin, die Studentin, Täterin, but die Deutsche.*

- Nouns ending in *-er*, when referring to people but, *die Jungfer, die Mutter, die Schwester, die Tochter, das Fenster.*

- Names of alcoholic drinks: *der Wein, der Wodka,* but *das Bier*

- Names of mountains and lakes: *der Berg, der See,* but Germany's highest peak, *die Zugspitze* follows the rule for the feminine ending *-e*, and *die See* is the sea.

- Most rivers outside of Europe: *der Amazonas, der Kongo, der Mississippi*

- Most nouns ending in *-ich, -ling, -ist*: *Rettich, Sittich, Schädling, Frühling, Pazifist* (radish, parakeet, pest/parasite, spring, pacifist)

German Noun Gender: Feminine - DIE

Always FEMININE (die/eine):

- Nouns ending in the following suffixes: *-heit, -keit, -tät, -ung, -schaft* - Examples: *die Freiheit, Schnelligkeit, Universität, Zeitung, Freundschaft* (freedom, quickness, university, newspaper, friendship). These suffixes usually have a corresponding English suffix, such as -ness (*-heit, -keit*), -ty (*-tät*), -ship (*-schaft*).
- Nouns ending in *-ie*: *Drogerie, Geographie, Komödie, Industrie, Ironie* (often equal to words ending in -y in English)
- Names of aircraft, ships and motorbikes: *die Boeing 747, die Titanic, die BMW* (motorbike only; the car is *der BMW*). The *die* comes from *die Maschine,* which can mean plane, motorbike and engine. - Helpful reminder: Ships are often referred to as "she" in English.
- Nouns ending in *-ik*: *die Grammatik, Grafik, Klinik, Musik, Panik, Physik.*
- Borrowed (foreign) nouns ending in: *-ade, -age, -anz, -enz, -ette, -ine, -ion, -tur*: *Parade, Blamage* (shame), *Bilanz, Distanz, Frequenz, Serviette* (napkin), *Limonade, Nation, Konjunktur* (economic trend).
- Cardinal numbers: *eine Eins, eine Drei* (a one, a three)

Usually FEMININE (die/eine):

- Nouns ending in *-in* that pertain to female people, occupations, nationalities: *Amerikanerin, Studentin* (female

American, student), but *der Harlekin* and also many non-people words: *das Benzin, der Urin* (gasoline/petrol, urine).

- Most nouns ending in *-e*: *Ecke, Ente, Grenze, Pistole, Seuche* (corner, duck, border, pistol, epidemic), but *der Deutsche, das Ensemble, der Friede, der Junge* ([the] German, ensemble, peace, boy)
- Nouns ending in *-ei*: *Partei, Schweinerei* (party [political], dirty trick/mess), but *das Ei, der Papagei* (egg, parrot).
- Most types of flowers and trees: *Birke, Chrysantheme, Eiche, Rose* (birch, chrysanthemum, oak, rose), but *der Ahorn,* (maple), *das Gänseblümchen* (daisy), and the word for tree is *der Baum*
- Borrowed (foreign) nouns ending in *-isse, -itis, -ive*: *Hornisse, Initiative* (hornet, initiative)

German Noun Gender: Neuter - DAS

Always NEUTER (das/ein):

- Nouns ending in *-chen* or *-lein*: *Fräulein, Häuschen, Kaninchen, Mädchen* (unmarried woman, cottage, rabbit, girl/maiden)
- Infinitives used as nouns (gerunds): *das Essen, das Schreiben* (eating/food, writing)
- Almost all of the 112 known *chemical elements (das Aluminium, Blei, Kupfer, Uran, Zink, Zinn, Zirkonium, usw.*) - except for five that are masculine: *der Kohlenstoff* (carbon), *der Sauerstoff* (oxygen), *der Stickstoff* (nitrogen), *der Wasserstoff* (hydrogen), and *der Schwefel* (sulphur). Most •

of the elements end in *-ium*, a *das* ending.

- Names of hotels, cafés and theaters
- Names of colors used as nouns: *das Blau, das Rot* (blue, red)

Usually NEUTER (das/ein):

- Geographic place names (towns, countries, continents): *das Berlin, Deutschland, Brasilien, Afrika* (but countries, such as: *der Irak, der Jemen, die Schweiz, die Türkei, die USA* [plur.])
- Young animals and people: *das Baby, das Küken* (chick); but *der Junge* (boy).
- Most metals: *Aluminium, Blei, Kupfer, Messing, Zinn* (aluminium, lead, copper, brass, tin/pewter; but *die Bronze, der Stahl* - bronze, steel)
- Nouns ending in *-o*: *das Auto, Büro, Kasino, Konto (account), Radio, Veto, Video - Exceptions: die Avocado, die Disko, der Euro, der Scirocco, etc.*
- Fractions: *das/ein Viertel (¼), das/ein Drittel*, but *die Hälfte*, half.
- Most nouns starting with *Ge-*: *Genick, Gerät, Geschirr, Geschlecht, Gesetz, Gespräch* (back of the neck, device, dishes, sex/gender, law, conversation), but there are many exceptions, such as *der Gebrauch, der Gedanke, die Gefahr, der Gefallen, der Genuss, der Geschmack, der Gewinn, die Gebühr, die Geburt, die Geduld, die Gemeinde, die Geschichte*, and others)
- Most borrowed (foreign) nouns ending in *-ment*: *Ressentiment, Supplement* (but *der Zement, der/das Moment* [2 diff. meanings])

Most nouns ending in *-nis*: *Versäumnis* (neglect; but *die Erlaubnis, die Erkenntnis, die Finsternis*)

- Most nouns ending in *-tum* or *-um*: *Christentum, Königtum* (Christianity, kingship; but *der Irrtum, der Reichtum* - error, wealth)

Chapter 10

Possessiv-Pronomen

	Maskulin	Neutral	Feminin
ich	mein Freund meine Freunde	mein Buch meine Bücher	meine Uhr deine Uhren
du	dein Freund deine Freund	dein Buch deine Bucher	deine Uhr deine Uhren
er, es	sein Freund seine Freunde	sein Buch seine Bücher	seine Uhr seine Uhren
sie	ihr Freund ihre Freunde	ihr Buch ihre Bücher	ihre Uhr ihre Uhren
wir	unser Freund unsere Freunde	unser Buch unsere Bücher	unsere Uhr unsere Uhren
ihr	euer Freund eure Freunde	euer Buch euere Bücher	eure Uhr eure Uhren
sie	ihr Freund ihre Freunde	ihr Buch ihre Bücher	ihre Uhr ihre Uhren
Sie	Ihr Freund Ihre Freunde	Ihr Buch Ihre Bücher	Ihre Uhr Ihre Uhren

Exercises:

This is my guest.
Das ist **mein** Gast.
das ist maain gaast

This is her guest.
Das ist **ihr** Gast.
das ist ihr gaast

It is their guest.
Das ist **ihr** Gast.
das ist ihr gaast

Good Morning, Mr. Walter, how are your wife and children?
Guten Morgen, Herr Walter, wie geht es **Ihre** Frau und Kinder?
gutayn morgayn, hayr vaaltayr, vee gayht es ihray fraau unt kindayr

Good Day, Mr. Clark, how is your wife and your son?
Guetn Tag, Herr Clark, wie geht es **Ihre** Frau und **Ihr** Sohn?
gutayn taag, hayrr Claark, vee gayht es ihray fraau undt ihr zohn

Mr. Breuer helps his wife.
Herr Beuer hilft **seine** Frau.
hayr Breuayr hilft zaainay fraau

Richard does not smoke. Cigaratte is injurious for his health.
Richard raucht nicht. Zigaretten schaden **seine** Gesundheit.
rishaard raaukht nisht. Tsigaretayn shaadayn zaainay gezunthaait

Erika does not smoke too. Cigaratte is injurious for her health too.
Erika raucht auch nicht. Auch **ihre** Gesundheit schaden die Zigaretten.
erikaa raaukht aaukh nisht. Aaukh ihray gezunthaait shaadayn dee tsigaaraytayn

Chapter 11

Personal Pronomen

Nom.	Akk.	Dat.
ich	mich	mir
du	dich	dir
er	ihn	ihm
es	es	ihm
sie	sie	ihr
wir	uns	uns
ihr	euch	euch
sie	sie	ihnen
Sie	Sie	Ihnen

Exercises:

My father is visiting you.
Mein Vater kommt zu **dir**.
maain faatar komt tsu dear

The teacher is asking you and not me.
Der Lehrer fragt **dich** und nicht **mich**.
dayr layhrayr fraagt dish unt nisht mish

You have no time for me.
Du hast keine Zeit für **mich**.
du haast kaainay tsaait fuer mish

I work quite often with him.
Ich arbeite oft mit **ihm**.
ikh aarbaitay oft mit ihm

I am coming with her.
Ich komme mit **ihr**.
ikh komay mit ihr

You have two children. What should I bring for them?
Sie haben zwei Kinder. Was bringe ich ihnen **mit**.
zee haabayn tswaai kindayr. Vaas bringay ikh ihnayn mit

Chapter 12

How to tell time in German

1. An hour is divided up like a pie into quarters (**viertel**) and halves (**halb**).
2. For “half past,” you say **halb** and the next hour. “Halb acht” = 7:30, i.e., half (way to) eight.
3. After is **nach**. “Es ist zehn nach zwei” = 2:10 (It’s ten after two).
4. For „quarter past,“ you say **Viertel nach**: „Viertel nach neun“ = 9:15.
5. To or before is **vor** (FOR). „Viertel vor zwei“ = 1:45. „Zehn vor elf“ = 10:50.
6. English „o’clock“ is **Uhr** in German. „Es ist fünf Uhr“ = 5:00 (five o’clock).
7. For precise times, you say **Uhr** between the hour and the minutes: „zehn Uhr zwölf“ = 10:12.
8. For many common situations (timetables, TV guides), Germans use 24-hour (military) time.
9. Add 12 to a pm time to get the 24-hour form: 2 pm + 12 = 14.00 (vierzehn Uhr).
10. To express 24-hour time, be precise: “zwanzig Uhr neun” = 20.09 = 8:09 pm.

Exercises

1. Practise these words aloud.

English	German	Pronunciation
Yes	ja	yaa
Year	Jahr	yaar
Young	jung	yung
June	Juni	fearyaa
Father	Vater	faatar
Full	voll	fol
Four	vier	fear
From	von	fon
Water	Wasser	vaa-sar
Wind	Wind	vint
World	Welt	velt
What	was	vaas
When	wenn	ven
We	wir	vear
As	wie	vee
Warm	warm	vaarm
Ten	zehn	tsayn
Twelve	zwölf	tswoelf
March	März	maerts

December	Dezember	detsember
To count	zählen	tsaylayn
Cigarette	Zigarette	tsigarete
Son	Sohn	zon
September	September	zeptember
Rose	Rose	ro-ze
Music	Musik	mu-zik
To tell	sagen	zaagayn
To sing	singen	zingen
To sit	sitzen	zitsen
To see	sehen	zehen
School	Schule	shoolay
Sister	Schwester	shwester
German	Deutsch	doiach
English	Englisch	aynglish
To wish	wünschen	vuenshen
Fresh	Frisch	frish
Student	Student	student
To speak	sprechen	sprekhen
Chair	Stuhl	stul
To stand	stehen	stehen

2.

This is Sanjana Gupta.
Sie heisst Sanjana Gupta.
zee haaist Sanjana Gupta

She comes from Banglore.
Sie kommt aus Banglore.
zee komt aaus banglore

She lives in Delhi.
Sie wohnt in Delhi.
zee vont in Delhi

She learns German.
Sie learnt Deutsch.
zee layrnt doiach

This is Thomas Wild.
Er heisst Thomas Wild.
ayr haaist thomaas vilt

He comes from Frankfurt.
Er kommt aus Frankfurt.
ayr komt aaus frankfoort

He lives in Delhi.
Er wohnt in Delhi.
ayr vont in Delhi

He learns Hindi.
Er learnt Hindi.
ayr layrnt Hindi

This is Dino Botta.
Er heisst Dino Botta.
ayr haaist Dino Botta

He comes from Rom.
Er kommt aus Rom.
ayr komt aaus Rom

He lives in Bonn.
Er wohnt in Bonn.
ayr vont in Bon

He learns German.
Er learnt Deutsch.
ayr layrnt doiach

This is Monika Mai.
Sie heisst Monika Mai.
zee haaist Monika Maai

She comes from Vienna.
Sie kommt aus Wien.
zee komt aaus veen

She lives in Humburg.
Sie wohnt in Berlin.
zee vont in Berlin

She learns Italian.
Sie learnt Italienisch.
zee layrnt Itaaliaynish

3. Song/Lied (leed)

German is super and not difficult.
Deutsch ist super und nicht schwer
doiach ist zupayr unt nisht shwayr

Gitarre, Trompete, Saxophon,
Computer, Radio und Telefon.
gitaaray, trompete, zaxophon,
computer, raadio unt telefon

Tennis, Windsurfen, Basketball,
Trapez, Zylinder und Oval.
Tenis, vintsoorfen, baasketbal,
traapets, tsuilindayr unt oval

Salat, Hamburger, Makkaroni,
Elefant, Giraffe und Pony.
Zalaat, hamburgayr, makaroni,
elefaant, giraafay unt poni
Präposition, Verb, Adjektiv,
Pistole, Killer und Detektiv,
praepozitsion, verb, adyektiv,
pistole, kiler unt detektiv

Alles normal,
deutsch ist super, international.
Alays normaal,
doiach ist zupayr, internaatsionaal

4. We Maker/ Wir Macher (vear maakhar)

I do sport.
Ich mache Sport.
ikh maakhay Sport

You do Yoga.
Du machst Yoga.
du maakhst yoga

He does politics.
Er macht Politik.
ayr maakht politik

She does Theater.
Sie macht Theater.
zee maakht thayaatayr

We all make mistakes.
Wir alle machen Fehler.
vear alay maakhayn fayhlayr

You guys are doing stupidities.
Ihr alle macht Dummheiten.
ihr alay maakht doomhaaitayn

They all are doing nonsense.
Sie alle machen Quatsch.
zee alay maakhayn kuaatch

5. Small Dialogue/ Kleiner Dialog (klaainayr deeaalog)

Where are you going?
Wohin gehst du?
vohin gayst du

I am going to the mess.
Ich gehe in die Mensa.
ikh gehe in dee menzaa

What is there in the mess today?
Was gibt es heute in der Mensa.
vaas gibt es heutay in dayr menzaa

Today there is Bratwurst in der Mensa.
In der mensa gibt es heute bratwurst.
in dayr menzaa gibt es heutay braatwoorst

Then I will come along.
Dann komme ich mit.
dan komay ikh mit

6. Familie Album:

Is it your family?
Ist das deine Familie?
ist das daainay faamilee

Yes. Here, this is my father.
Ja. Hier, das ist mein Vater.
Yaa. Heear, das ist maain faatar

This is your father? He is still young!
Das ist dein Vater? Er ist noch jung!
das ist daain faatar? Ayr ist nokh yoong

No, he is already sixty.
Nein, er ist schon sechzig.-
naain, ayr ist shon zechtsig

And your mother?
Und deine Mutter?
unt daainay mutar
Here this is her. She is 55.
Hier, das ist sie. Sie ist 55.
heear, das ist zee. Zee ist 55

Do you have brothers and sisters?
Hast du Geschwister?
haast du geshwistayr

7. Where / What / Who? whom (wo/woher/wohin/was/wen/wem oder wer)

Where is the table?
Wo steht der Tisch?
vo shteht dayr tish

From where comes Mr. Wilson?
Woher kommt Herr Wilson?
vohayr komt hayr vilson

Where is Sanjay flying to?
Wohin fliegt Sanjay?
vohin fleegt Sanjay

Where is the garden?
Wo ist der Garten?
vo ist dayr gaartayn

From where has the latter come?
Woher kommt der Brief?
vohayr komt dayr breef

Whom are you looking for?
Wen suchst du?
ven zookhst du

Yes, I have two brothers.
Ja, ich habe zwei Brüder.
Yaa, ikh haabay tswaai bruedayr

Here, this is Gerd.
Hier, das ist Gerd.
heear, das ist gayrd

He still goes to school, he is sixteen.
Er geht noch zur Schule. Er ist sechzehn.
ayr gayt nokh tsooar shoolay. Ayr ist zekstsayn

And this is Martin.
Und das ist Martin.
unt das ist maartin

And this? Are they your grandparents?
Und das? Sind das deine grosseltern?
Unt das? Zeent das daainay groseltayrn?
Yes. They are very old.
Ja. Sie sind schon sehr alt.
yaa. Zee zint shon zayr aalt

My grandfather is 85, my grandmother is 83.
Mein grossvater ist 85, meine grossmutter ist 83.
Maainay grosfaatar ist aakhtuntfuenftsig, maainay grosmutar ist draaiuntfuenftsig

What is the teacher asking?
Was fragt der Lehrer?
vaas fraagt dayr lehrar

Whom do you help?
Wem hilfst du?
vem hilfst du

What is cheap?
Was ist billig?
vaas ist billish

8. Yes-No-emphatic yes / Ja-Nein-Doch

Are you going Home? No, I am staying here.
Gehst du nach Hause? **Nein,** ich bleibe hier.
gayst du naakh haauzay? Naain, ikh blaaibay heear
Do you have my copy? Yes, but not here.
Hast du mein heft? **Ja,** aber nicht hier.
haast du maain heft? Yaa, aabayr nisht heear

Is not Claudia going to Heidelberg? Yes, but not today.
Fährt Claudia nicht nach Heidelberg? **Doch,** aber nicht heute.
Faert claaudeeaa nisht naakh haaidaylberg? Dokh, aabayr nisht heutay
Are not you coming in the evening today? Yes, I am coming at seven in the evening today.
Kommst du heute abend nicht? **Doch,** ich komme heute abend um 7.00 Uhr.
Komst du heute aabent nisht? Dokh ikh kome heute aabent oom zeebäyn ooar

Don't you guys drink beer? Yes, we drink lot of beer.
Trinkt ihr kein Bier? **Doch,** wir trinken viel Bier.
Trinkt eear kaain beear? Dokh vear trinken feel beear